ICE HOCKEY

ICE HOCKEY

A FAN'S VIEW

STEVE FLEMMING

Matador
9 Priory Business Park,
Wistow Road, Kibworth Beauchamp,
Leicestershire. LE8 0RX
Tel: (+44) 116 279 2299
Fax: (+44) 116 279 2277
Email: books@troubador.co.uk
Web: www.troubador.co.uk/matador

ISBN 978 1785890 352

British Library Cataloguing in Publication Data.
A catalogue record for this book is available from the British Library.

Printed and bound by CPI Group (UK) Ltd, Croydon, CR0 4YY
Typeset in 12pt Aldine by Troubador Publishing Ltd, Leicester, UK

Matador is an imprint of Troubador Publishing Ltd

CONTENTS

CHAPTER 1

INTRODUCTION

On Saturday 1st November 1986 I was taken by friends from Stoney Creek, Ontario, to my first live ice hockey game; it just happened to be at the legendary Maple Leaf Gardens in Toronto. It gets better... It was an NHL game, the Toronto Maple Leafs v Detroit Red Wings.

On Saturday, 3rd December 2011, I travelled to Winnipeg, Manitoba, to see the Winnipeg Jets v New Jersey Devils. This particular venue allowed me to complete, in full, all the NHL arenas (37) including teams which have moved to new facilities.

I have become an avid fan of the game and have travelled far and wide to view different levels of the sport. All these years have quite simply been a personal experience in the world of watching ice hockey. It has been a great journey, so I just had to attempt to re-cap it all and share some of the memories; there seemed no better way to do it than in print.

The book is divided into chapters covering the different competitions that form part of the game played throughout the world. This includes domestically and internationally from the annually held World Championships to the Winter Olympics and the European club competition, the Continental Cup, in addition to bring things right up to date, the Champions Hockey League.

When I came to do the research for the book it came as a surprise even to me just how many games I had watched and places I had actually travelled to. I have visited all the major league venues in three countries to date, the NHL in North America, the DEL in Germany and the EIHL in our own country Great Britain. Overall I have covered 116 ice arenas in 19 countries, I have attended 19 World Championships, 8 Continental Cup tournaments and just the 1 Winter Olympics with 3 qualifiers.

For almost 30 years now I have remained a committed fan of the Nottingham Panthers. I have devoted a section divided into three parts to cover this. It will also include the top ice hockey league in Great Britain starting back in the Heineken sponsored years, touching on the Super League through to the present day of the Elite League. The Great Britain national team is covered in more detail in the World Championships section.

All of the games I have witnessed most certainly do not make me an expert on the game; there are other fans out there who have watched the game longer and covered the same ground and more. This book is just about my experiences and my opinions, and above all to describe how fortunate I have been to have done all of this and to have met some great people along the way.

INTRODUCTION

Finally to any fellow ice hockey enthusiasts out there who may take the time to read this book, I do hope it provokes some past memories for you.

CHAPTER 2

THE NATIONAL HOCKEY LEAGUE (NHL)

When I started watching the NHL in 1986 there were 21 teams involved in the league. Today, of course, there are 30 teams, some of which have moved cities, others to new facilities. When I attended the game in Winnipeg in December 2011, I had then completed the full set of NHL clubs which total 37 arenas. Admittedly it has taken a while. Unfortunately my job was always demanding and time and money was always a consideration. It was only in 1999 that I really decided that I should try and visit all the arenas. It is a poor effort really when you consider my wife, Karen, only attended her first NHL game in Vancouver in January 2007, and eight years on she needs to visit just one more arena for her to complete all 30 clubs.

Now all this pales into insignificance when you consider a gentleman from Los Angeles (Andre Delsol), who is now officially in the Guinness Book of World Records for visiting 30 different NHL arenas to cover 30 games inside just 29 days. What excellent planning! Andre does have his own website www.hockeyonthefly.

com. He actually wrote an article about me on the site titled The Godfather!

So back to Saturday, 1st November 1986. Now prior to this I had shown little and no interest in ice hockey. I knew little about the sport although I did recall a famous game during the Winter Olympics in 1980 at Lake Placid between the USA and the USSR. Also in my local papers, the *Nottingham Evening Post* and *Football Post*, there were always reports on the Nottingham Panthers. My recollection was of high-scoring games and quite a few players named 'Keward'; strange what sticks in your mind.

Arriving that evening in Toronto for the game against the Detroit Red Wings my first impression was of a real buzz in the atmosphere; an air of expectancy, bars were packed around Carlton Street and tills were ringing in the Leafs' shop. There were ticket touts everywhere (known locally as 'scalpers'). It is illegal of course but it still happens everywhere. Maple Leaf Gardens was built in 1930; the front exterior of the building reminded me of an old cinema. Inside it was a little more grand – food and drink was available everywhere. This was obviously a complete night out for the fans. The game was sold out (it always was and still is). We had great seats, a top view of all the action. Before the start both the Canadian and American national anthems were sung. Already the evening was providing me with a completely different view of a sporting event. When you grow up watching football and cricket it leaves you with a certain mind-set attributed to those sports. Also attending football games in the eighties carried a health warning with so much trouble around, so it was to become a refreshing change to follow a sport where the majority of fans mix well with each other and leave the aggression to the players on the ice.

The game started and it soon became apparent, even to me, that these two teams did not like each other. A fight soon broke out, I had been warned this might happen as the Leafs and Red Wings had history. The fight though seemed a little staged, a lot of holding, grabbing and pulling of shirts amongst a few punches being thrown. I thought perhaps this part might be like the WWF wrestling but I would never have mentioned this to my friends though. I mean, they were Canadian and I was in their town. Actually the following day on reading a report in the Toronto Sun I found out the Leafs' player involved in the fight had broken his ankle when the two players fell on the ice – I have never queried a fight since! My friends spent the evening trying to explain what was happening and some of the rules (the very same thing I would also do on numerous occasions many years later). The game was fast and furious so I struggled a little to understand player changes, stoppages for icing and some of the penalties, which did not seem clear to me. There seemed to be a lot happening off the puck. Also in those days you could not pass the puck forward over two lines, and my immediate thoughts were these officials must certainly earn their money!

Now the Leafs' fans have changed little over the years. That evening was the first time I heard the term 'sucked'. It seemed the referee, all of Detroit and even some of the Leafs' own players 'sucked'. Recently I visited the Air

Canada Centre, the Leafs' new home, and guess what? Everyone still 'sucked'. Of course the Leafs' fans will readily explain that they have a reason over many years to complain about the team, as they are usually playing golf at play-off time. In fact the last time this famous club won the Stanley Cup was over 45 years ago!

I do regret not retaining a match programme from my first NHL game, but my memory of certain players remained as I was to visit many more times as watching the Leafs seemed to become the norm. Toronto beat Detroit 2-0 on the night. Some of the Leafs' players on the roster were big names at that time: Wendel Clark, a real fans' favourite, played for 15 years until a back problem was to limit his effectiveness later in his career; Todd Gill, a defender who went on to play 1,100 NHL games; Gary Leeman who scored over 200 goals for the Leafs and later played in Europe in the DEL with the Hannover Scorpions; Borje Salming, a Leaf legend from Sweden who played for 16 seasons with the Leafs. Also on the roster was Derek Laxdal, a forward, who played 50 times in Toronto. He will also be familiar to fans in Great Britain where he played over 200 games for the Nottingham Panthers, Sheffield Steelers and Humberside Hawks.

For Detroit there were two players who became real legends: Steve Yzerman who played his entire NHL career with the Red Wings (1,700 games) and the late Bob Probert. Bob was known mainly for his enforcer role but actually he still had a place in Leaf history despite never playing for them – he scored the last ever goal at the Gardens on 13 February 1999 for Chicago in a 6-2 victory. Strange the very first opponents in 1931 at the Gardens were also the Blackhawks who won on that day 2-1.

Between 1932 and 1967 the Leafs won 11 Stanley Cups and even Elvis played the Gardens in 1957, but unfortunately both he and the Leafs have now left the building.

That night in Toronto had been quite enthralling. I needed to experience more of this sport, so on my return to the UK I started to attend games at the old arena in Nottingham. This was the start of a 28-year period of watching British ice hockey.

During the future years on my return to Toronto I had the opportunity to see many games at the MLG. I remember seeing some teams that would not continue in their present format, such as the Quebec Nordiques. My memory will always be of Guy Lafleur skating for the French side with no helmet (not compulsory at that time). I did visit Quebec City in the nineties but Joe Sakic and the Nordiques had already left town due to financial issues. In fact the very next season after they left (1995/96) they won the Stanley Cup but as the Colorado Avalanche and also again in 2001. To this day there is no NHL club in Quebec City but I did notice at a couple of recent NHL games some banners with 'Bring back the Nordiques'. Unfortunately the NHL has stated that they have no plans to extend the current 30 teams.

I saw the Winnipeg Jets on a couple of occasions; again though lack of support and finance would see the team relocated to Arizona. They became the Phoenix Coyotes and firstly played at the America West Arena but would later move to a new arena in Glendale. In 2011 I visited Atlanta to see the Thrashers (this became their final season) before they moved to become the Jets in Winnipeg, and of course this was to become my final stop in December 2011 to complete my journey. To anyone other than an ice hockey fan all of this would be confusing in the extreme.

I managed to see the Minnesota North Stars in Toronto before they moved to Dallas. There is, of course, now a new NHL team in Minneapolis known as 'the Wild' who play in St Paul. I remember also watching the Hartford Whalers in Toronto but poor support contributed to the Whalers' demise.

On one of my many trips to Toronto (around 20 visits over the years), I managed to take a couple of side journeys to watch other clubs. A drive over to Buffalo was a regular haunt for Canadians just to shop or buy cheaper fuel. My goal though was to see the Buffalo Sabres. Now crossing the border at Niagara Falls can be a lengthy process if you have a different passport, i.e. British. The trick here is always to be friendly and polite – it works! The arena at that time was the Auditorium (Aud), another older building from 1940. The capacity was a little on the low side at just over 14,000, not enough for an NHL team. The Sabres were to move later to a brand new arena and the Aud was demolished in 1996. That evening during the 1987/88 season was a game against the Montreal Canadiens. It was a pulsating affair won 5-3 by the Sabres. There were some real legends on view: for Buffalo, Dave Andreychuk who played 1,800 games and

Pierre Turgeon with over 500 goals. Also on the Sabres roster was Ken Priestlay who will be very well known in the UK as he was part of the Grand Slam winning season in 1996 with the Sheffield Steelers. Priestlay played 182 NHL games scoring 67 goals. He also won two Stanley Cup rings with the Pittsburgh Penguins. For Montreal, Patrick Roy, a real goalkeeping legend. He won four Stanley Cups, played ten years in Montreal and eight years in Colorado. I was indeed to catch up with Roy at the Winter Olympics in Nagano, Japan where he was playing for Team Canada. Guy Cabonneau who played 13 years with the Canadiens and Chris Chelios another NHL legend were also on view.

My other trip was actually to Montreal, around a five to six-hour drive from Toronto. It is a great city to visit. Sports teams though have come and gone. The Montreal Expo's were a major league baseball team (one of only two in Canada) but lack of support was to see the team relocated to Washington DC (now the Nationals). The Montreal Canadiens have never had that problem; quite the opposite in fact, obtaining a ticket for games is an issue. The game I saw was at the Forum against the Detroit Red Wings. The Forum is a really old arena from 1926 and apparently the Beatles played there in 1964. It had flags galore hanging from the rafters, many acclaiming their Stanley Cup triumphs (24 in total). I felt I was surrounded by history. The Canadiens have now moved to a new facility – the Bell Centre. The good thing about the arenas in Toronto and Montreal are that they are in good downtown locations.

During the Nineties I continued to travel to North America when the opportunity allowed. One of my favourite destinations is Scottsdale, Arizona, just outside of Phoenix. As previously mentioned the Winnipeg Jets moved to Arizona in 1996 and became the Phoenix Coyotes. At first they used the America West Centre, a good location right downtown next to the baseball stadium. The Centre was actually the home of the Phoenix Suns (basketball) so it had not been built for ice hockey. I always thought the corners looked a little odd. I saw a few games there and encountered a strange experience during an evening in the 1990s when Phoenix played against the Boston Bruins. I took my parents to the game (their first ever). I had explained how the fans were: no problems, easy parking, good seats, good food – it was all good, but wait… after a narrow win for the Coyotes and on the final whistle fighting broke out in the crowd! A group of Boston and Phoenix fans squared up to each other. On his return from the toilets, my father reported wall-to-wall fighting in there also. He commented it was just like being at football. I was quite shocked and disappointed. Fortunately, in all my years I have only witnessed a couple of other similar incidents.

The Coyotes moved to a new facility just outside Glendale in 2003. Well, actually, it's in the middle of nowhere but it's now built up with shops, restaurants, bars and a hotel. The Arizona Cardinals (American Football) also play at the complex. I like it there especially if you stay at the hotel – you can even go to your room during the period breaks. The Yard House is on site and one of my favourite bar/restaurant chains in North America – and there is something quite nice in early December when you can go to a game in shorts. Unfortunately the Coyotes have always had a problem with a lack of support. I have spoken to some season ticket holders who are happy with the new arena but not where it is, quite a distance from Phoenix and Scottsdale with little or no public transport, so driving is the only option. I do hope with all the rumours around that the Coyotes do manage to stay in Arizona. In fact the team is now known as the 'Arizona Coyotes'. I guess this may be part of a new initiative to improve the club's image and support. One player I do like in the team is Shane Doan who has played his entire career with the franchise, moving from Winnipeg. In fact he was given a warm welcome back in Winnipeg on his return. He did comment how strange it felt though playing for the Coyotes against the Jets.

My next venture would take me to the West of Canada – to Vancouver. This is a really nice city. My wife and I always visit a restaurant there called CinCin's, one of our favourite places to dine in North America. Also we like to stay at the Pan Pacific or Waterfront Hotels; both are a short walk from the Rogers Arena where the Vancouver Canucks now play. However, my first visit was in 1993 when they played at the Pacific Coliseum, which is in the Hastings area, a little way out of the city. I arrived at the airport on the day of the game. Getting downtown was always difficult but nowadays a rail link is in place thanks to the Olympics. After checking in at the Waterfront Hotel I found out you could purchase a ticket for the game in Sears. No problem so I thought – it was only mid-afternoon – plenty of time. I remember the puzzled look the lady gave me when I asked to purchase a ticket in the store. "Yes, we still have a couple of tickets here but you will miss the start," she told me. I said just how far is it as I have four hours to get there. She laughed and pointed out it was a 4.30pm start – the 7.30pm I had seen was indeed 'eastern time'! Oh dear! Red faced I ran for a bus to Hastings. More embarrassment – no change for the bus, but the driver let me on anyway. It seemed miles (only six actually), but other fans got on so I thought no problem on time, except arriving late for games in North America seems to be fashionable for some reason. I made it just as 'Oh Canada' finished but then promptly sat in the wrong seat and even when I moved I wasn't sure I was in the right place. It had all been too hectic and I still felt quite stupid! I think the game was in the second period before I started to enjoy it. The Calgary Flames were the visitors. I recall seeing a penalty shot for the first time scored by Gino Odjick of the Canucks (v. Mike Vernon of Calgary), which brought the house down. It was quite a rowdy evening/afternoon at the game. I noticed many fans had smuggled in hip flasks! Trevor Linden played for the Canucks and still did in 2007 when I took Karen to her first match. He did though have a four-year spell away from Vancouver. Overall he played 1,500 NHL games and is now the president of hockey operations in Vancouver.

The following season (1993/94) Vancouver reached the Stanley Cup final. It went to game seven against the New York Rangers who won the cup on 14th June 1994 in Madison Square Garden. The defeat sparked off rioting back in Vancouver. Then in 2011 (17 years on) the very same thing happened when yet again the Canucks lost game seven of the final, this time at home to Boston. Riots broke out after the game almost like a copycat of 1994. This time though with today's communication networks the whole world saw it and it painted ice hockey in a poor light, a great shame for such a lovely city. Fortunately I was not present on either evening.

The mid-nineties took me to Calgary. This was the first time that I would see Theoren Fleury. I actually went twice over a three-year period and for me he stood out on the ice. He seemed to be so much quicker and more powerful than other players, yet he was only 5' 6" tall. His career and off-ice issues have been well documented of course, but it was still nice to see him play again though some years later (2005/06) for the Belfast Giants in the Elite League in the UK. In contrast to Fleury, at both games in Calgary I watched another power forward, Jarome Iginla, young in those days but eventually he spent 17 years with the Flames. Perhaps things might have turned out different for Fleury if he had been able to stay longer in Calgary. Unfortunately the Flames traded him to Colorado, and following a brief stay he signed a three-year contract with the New York Rangers. The Saddledome in Calgary is quite unique in its external features. Shaped like a saddle it is on the edge of the city – walkable or by local tram. On my first visit I bought a ticket outside from a couple that had season tickets. It was nice to sit with them and get an insight into the Flames. What nice people too. They insisted on taking me to a bar called Dusty's after the game for wings – a proper hockey night! There was also live country music at the venue which was a real bonus for me. Sadly, in December 2011 on my return to Calgary, Dusty's was gone!

In 1999, along with a friend, I travelled across Canada, flying in and out of cities just to watch ice hockey. It had been put to me that perhaps I should consider visiting all the NHL arenas. This would not be easy living in the UK. Also most of the arenas I had visited already had moved to new facilities – dedicated tours would be necessary to do it! This particular trip started in late January 1999 in Vancouver. I started out with a bad cold – not a good idea when tackling the Canadian winter. Also it is not advisable to try and watch a game following a long flight. On this occasion it was Vancouver v Chicago, a really good match ending 3-2 to the Canucks. Unfortunately by the third period I was struggling to stay awake. The next day was free so a chance to hire a car and take it on the ferry to Victoria (which is certainly worth a visit). The evening back in Vancouver left us with many choices of bars and restaurants. We went to an oyster bar and sat across from Tom Berenger who apparently was filming in the area. The following day saw a visit from the Ottawa Senators. No tiredness issues on that evening, which started at a bar connected to the Sandman Hotel, a short walk from the arena. It's a proper hockey bar with large split screens showing games at different stages from various other NHL locations. It's always good to talk to local fans about their team.

The GM Place (now the Rogers Arena) is a good venue with seats in the second tier near the front being the best view. I always think that most arenas in North America are built with seats at lower levels (first tier, 100 level) not being steep enough, more set back. They are not all like this but many are and the view is not the best. I like to be close to the action so centre ice (200 level) in the first four rows if you can get tickets are what I aim for. Back in the nineties I used to try and book tickets ahead by calling the club concerned. Ticketmaster – online bookings – I do not believe existed at that time!

Ottawa won a tight game 1-0. We ran into the Senators again in Edmonton so more on them later. The Canucks had some great names on their roster at that time including Mark Messier who had lifted the Stanley Cup on that evening back in 1994 at Madison Square Garden. As the New York Rangers Captain, Messier played almost 2000 NHL games scoring 800 goals and was involved in six Stanley Cup wins during his career. Todd Bertuzzi, unfortunately he was injured during my visit although I did see him on other occasions, was eventually traded by the Canucks to Florida in 2006.

Donald Brashear was also on the team and he was used mainly as an 'enforcer'. Finally Markus Naslund from Sweden who played 12 seasons in Vancouver, eight years of which he was captain. He appeared in five All Star Games and became a real fan favourite.

The following day was again free so this time with no NHL to watch we headed to northern British Columbia and Prince George. It's about a 90-minute flight. A taxi from the airport showed we had run into the Canadian winter – snow and ice everywhere. The driver payed no attention, just another day of sliding everywhere.

The town, well... not a one-horse town but small. There seemed to be an abundance of furniture stores and hairdressers. The hotel was great, inexpensive and connected to a casino (I was bound to finish the evening in there). Prince George Cougars play in the Western Hockey League (WHL). The evening game was against Portland. Players in this league are usually younger and looking to be drafted to a NHL franchise. The arena was probably walkable from downtown but not with pavements steeped in snow and ice. A taxi was called. A nice, smart arena with a capacity of 7,000, I would probably guess 5,500 were at the game and a good fast-paced game it was. Now to be honest I took little notice of the players' names on view that evening. I would not have heard of any in that league. However, on rechecking the roster I note two players for the Cougars from that night have played in the Elite League – Mike Bayrack and Tom Wedderburn.

Back to the NHL and a flight to Calgary (via Vancouver). One of the great values of that trip was purchasing an Air Canada flight pass which for each flight was $50. You will not find these kinds of tickets available now! Calgary was cold and brisk but no snow. The International Hotel was a place I had stayed before and a perfect location. Like most Canadian cities all transport downtown is by bus or taxi. A late lunch was had and on to the Saddledome, an easy find for me this time. The game was against the newcomers to the league – the Nashville Predators. The game ended 2-2 after overtime (penalty shots had not been introduced at that time), stand out players on the day were Theoren Fluery and Corey Stillman (Calgary), and Cliff Ronning

(Nashville). Actually it's a wonder I even managed to see the game as prior to the start I purchased a glass of wine, however, this is cowboy country and the Saddledome staff are only used to pouring pints of beer, therefore I was promptly poured a pint of wine. I did not return for a second glass.

Back to Calgary airport and a flight on a Dash 8, a small hopper plane up to Edmonton. It took one hour – just time for coffee and bourbon biscuits! It's a good bus ride downtown and the snow and ice were back and it was minus 17 degrees. The hotel backs onto a shopping mall which was so hot inside you almost fainted. Rexall Place is a short tram ride from the centre, a good bar/restaurant is just over the road and we had seats low down on the blue line. Next to us sat Wade Redden's father (Wade was a defender who played for Ottawa). He gave us an insight into how hard his son had to work as a youngster on his skating, fitness and his build. He had to sacrifice a lot of his early social life but obviously it all proved worthwhile to make it to the NHL. Wade also played for Team Canada. The game was OK, not the best, but still a high level of skill on show. It ended in another 2-2 draw in front of 14,487 spectators (86% full). As always there were some top players on view. For Ottawa: Marian Hossa, Sammy Salo, Vinny Prospal and Alexei Yashin. For Edmonton: Marty McSorley, Bill Guerin and Ryan Smyth who was a real legend with the club and retired at the end of the 2013/14 season.

It was during the 1980s that the Oilers were at their peak winning the Stanley Cup five times between 1984 and 1990, so called the 'Dynasty Years'. Icing for the Oilers at that time was 'The Great One', Wayne Gretzky, playing ten years in Edmonton scoring 1,773 points until the trade in 1988 to Los Angeles which shocked the world of hockey. Gretzky went on to play 20 seasons in the NHL totalling 2,857 points, which increased to over 3,000 when you factor in his early career (WHL) and representing Canada. His statistics and individual awards are quite unbelievable.

The next day's flight took me back to Toronto. It has always seemed like a second home to me, a chance to have a Friday night on the town – bars and restaurants on Front Street are always worth a visit. The following day was quite nostalgic – 6th February 1999. Maple Leaf Gardens held an open day so I just had to go. You could skate on the ice, visit the players' areas, press room etc. The last Leafs game would be played there the following week. It all seemed rather sad but times move on.

Now it seems the next part was where my planning had gone a little wrong. I had thought the St John Maple Leafs were playing that evening in Toronto (they sometimes did) but not on that occasion, and the thought of a Saturday night without hockey in Canada was not on, so a quickly arranged flight to Montreal was called for. We arrived in thick snow. We stayed at the Days Inn just a short walk from the Bell Centre, the Canadiens home nowadays. The game was against Buffalo (again), our seats were very high up as we were lucky to get them at the last minute really. The Canadian national anthem was partly sung in French, just a reminder you were in Quebec. Before the game, a capacity crowd raised the roof when a true Canadian legend came onto the ice – Maurice (Rocket) Richard. It was announced that he would receive an award from the NHL for 50 goals in 50 NHL games. He achieved this back in 1945. The game was fast and furious just the same as the previous clashes I had seen between these two sides. The Canadiens edged the game 3-2, Mark Recchi scored one of the goals for Montreal, and fans' favourite Saku Koivu played on the night. Fortunately the Finn was later able to overcome a cancer scare in order to continue his career. On the same night playing for the Buffalo Sabres was Paul Kruse who later played in the British ISL for Sheffield and Belfast. A visit to the Montreal Casino seemed a perfect way to complete the trip. Unfortunately overnight my cold turned to flu. At breakfast I was shaking so following a flight back to Toronto we managed to catch an early flight home to the UK.

The next few years proved to be a little sparse on the NHL front. Travel to North America became more difficult following the quite dreadful events on 11th September 2001. Some airlines went through and others merged. The outcome was less choice and flexibility coupled with increased costs. In addition to that security would obviously be much tighter with longer delays. International and domestic air travel would no longer be a simple journey and quite understandably so.

I returned to the States in October 2002. First and foremost it was to fulfil an ambition of completing a marathon, which I did in Lake Tahoe, Nevada. When I say complete, I mean I walked the marathon in seven hours plus (it was a difficult course!), and without some help from friends I would have given up at 18 miles due to blisters as some did. Following a few days in Las Vegas to relax a couple of us booked a flight to Los Angeles departing early afternoon. We had booked tickets for the evening game at the Honda Centre in Anaheim – The Ducks v the Los Angeles Kings. However, after several hours delay the flight was cancelled. The next flight would arrive after the game had already started. Anaheim is more than 20 miles from the Los Angeles airport so it became clear we would miss the game. I tried to re-book and fly to Orange County but it's only a small airport and no hire cars were available. We did miss the game and lost the price of the tickets although America West gave us vouchers for another flight in the future.

The following evening we did make it to the Staples Centre for the game Kings v Colorado. There is a Holiday Inn close by so you can walk to the arena. Nowadays though the area around Staples is all changed with a downtown theme of LA Live. Bars, restaurants, hotels, entertainment everywhere – it is an excellent location. The Staples Centre is, however, not the best viewing arena. You really need to sit in the lower level (100) but not towards the front. The second tier level all seemed to be corporate seats and executive boxes. I guess this is in keeping with the area (NBA also).

Our seats on the evening were fairly central but way back at the top level, not my choice but ticket availability and cost dictate. Before the game everyone arrives early – you have to have your photo taken next to Wayne Gretzky's statue! There is a great lounge area with split screens showing all games taking place. I counted nine on that evening. The food was excellent and there is a really good bar atmosphere for pre-game. The club shop was heaving on the night. For all this though the Kings have found success hard to come by over the years. Joe Sakic and the Colorado Avalanche were the visitors and the game made up for the previous night. The Av's were full of talent with Peter Forsberg, Milan Hejduk and Patrick Roy. All were of course part of the team that won the Stanley Cup in 2001. It was a tough game on the night but the Avs ran out 4-1 winners.

The Kings used to play at the Great Western Forum (until 1999). I am assured by people that went there that this was certainly not in a good part of Los Angeles. Gretzky played there after the famous trade from Edmonton in 1988 until his departure in 1996. Despite all my earlier trips to North America I never saw Gretzky play an NHL game. I did, however, watch him play live in 1998 for Team Canada at the Winter Olympics in Nagano, Japan.

I mentioned that prior to the LA visit I had been in Las Vegas. This is one of my all-time favourite destinations I have been to on many occasions. I have found ice hockey there (1993–1999). I watched the Las Vegas Thunder (IHL). They played at the Thomas and Mac Centre, a short ride from the Strip. Their coach at the time was Chris McSorley (later of course he coached the London Knights and Great Britain). The Thunder, I recall at that time, were not affiliated to any of the bigger franchises and eventually folded.

These days you will find a different team – the Las Vegas Wranglers (ECHL). They play at the Orleans Arena, a nice venue connected to the Orleans Hotel. Ice hockey, casino, bars, and restaurants all on the same site – what more could anybody want? Sometimes they even stage a midnight match. Unfortunately it was announced recently that the Wranglers have folded, what a great shame!

Due to my work commitments I have always been too busy at peak holiday times to take any time off. January was always a good month to book but you need to keep an eye on the weather when travelling. So, 11th January 2006, I caught a late flight from London Heathrow to Boston. I like this city – it's easy to get around either by walking or public transport. It's also very close to the airport. On a previous trip I had visited Fenway Park to watch the Red Sox baseball team. It was during the summer so all I could do was take a tour of the old Boston Gardens arena. I was never able to see a game there. The new arena is built right next to the old arena which was demolished in 1997. It was firstly named TD Banknorth Garden (now just TD Garden since 2009). It's right downtown next to the railway station.

I arrived late at the airport and stayed at the hotel on site. You just walk to check in from passport control, very user friendly indeed. It has a very good sports bar with excellent food. I sampled some of the local clam chowder soup with a couple of local beers.

The hotel offered a free ride to the local subway so the following morning I headed downtown. The subway trains were actually old trolley cars that run underground until you get to a more modern line. I walked all over Boston. It was brisk but no snow. I bought a ticket at the arena box office (lower corner view) and returned at 5pm for a pre-match meal/drink. A local police officer recommended a nice brewpub, good atmosphere with plenty of hockey fans. The evening game was against the Los Angeles Kings. Many fans had Manchester Monarch shirts on (AHL). They play in New Hampshire and are actually a farm team of the Kings. I have never understood this about the NHL having affiliated teams – AHL and ECHL – thousands of miles away. Boston fans were not happy. Joe Thornton had left town to join the San Jose Sharks. He had been the main goal scorer for the Bruins for many years, and this particular game just added to their frustration as the Kings built up a first period lead.

It got progressively worse for the Bruins as Alexander Frolov completed his hat trick for the Kings. The arena was half empty by this time and the Bruins keeper Andrew Raycroft was replaced by Tim Thomas while Mathew Garon posted a 30 shot shut out at the other end. LA won by a country mile 6-0. Playing on the night for the Kings was Luc Robitaille, a real legend for the club. Icing for Boston was Nick Boynton who had a 15 game spell for the Nottingham Panthers during the NHL lock-out season 2004/05.

The following morning it was just a few minutes' walk to check in for my flight to Toronto. On arrival I took a bus downtown where I indulged in a couple of glasses of wine on Front Street. I then caught the Go-Train to Oakville and a bus to Hamilton. I stayed with my friends in Stoney Creek. On Saturday evening it was a visit to Cops Coliseum, a place I had been to many times before. Back in the late eighties I actually spent a day with the staff there preparing for an evening event. It was a fascinating insight into the running of a multi-purpose arena. Also transforming the area from an ice pad into a wrestling event (WWF) was incredibly efficient, and I recall helping in a small way and even selling merchandise on the day.

Back to the evening in 2006 and an AHL game, Hamilton Bulldogs v Rochester Americans. Cops Coliseum holds about 12,000 and it was about half full for the game which turned out to be a physical affair. The Bulldogs are affiliated to Montreal so the colours match. The Rochester Americans ran out 5-3 winners on the night much to the delight of a coachload of their fans who had made the long trip. Icing for Rochester was Greg Jacina who joined the Nottingham Panthers in 2013/14.

I woke up during the night with raging toothache which refused to go away. The following morning when I caught the bus back to Toronto airport I still felt quite dreadful. I took some paracetamol and a brandy before my flight and slept all the way to Nashville. Arrival was late in the afternoon so it was a rush to get downtown to the hotel that on my arrival had lost my booking. I was not happy. However, the manager took my bag and assured me all would be sorted on my return. I walked to Nashville's arena which is situated right in the downtown area across from what seemed like a mile of bars and restaurants most playing live country music. I was pleased to stay two nights. It was a 7.30pm start against the Pittsburgh Penguins and I got lucky when the box office released some extra seats six rows from the front lower level for only $25. I doubt I ever paid less for an NHL ticket.

My toothache issue was long gone when part of a tooth came out whilst watching the game. How strange! If you ever needed something to take your mind off a problem well Nashville against Pittsburgh on that night certainly did it, an excellent end to end game with the best atmosphere I have encountered in the NHL so far created by the Predator fans with a few Penguins there also. Nashville took control with goals from Scott Walker (two), his first game after 33 out through injury, Paul Kariya and Adam Hall. At this stage they had led 5-1, however, Pittsburgh hit back with three goals but fell just short in a frantic finish, Thomas Vokoun in goal for Nashville faced 40 shots in the 5-4 win. Also playing for the Predators was rising star Shea Weber and also Steve Sullivan who would certainly make my top 10 NHL list; great speed, awareness and stick handling. For the Penguins, Sidney Crosby and veteran Ziggy Palffy stood out.

A second night in Nashville allowed me to visit the Country Hall of Fame and several of the aforementioned bars. Back on track though the following day with a lunchtime flight to Denver. The airport there used to be at Stapleton, which is miles from downtown, now they have built a new facility even further away. It cost $70 each way by taxi or $20 by bus. My hotel (Adams Mark) was right downtown. There was a free transit that runs in the main area. I found the centre of Denver to be quite a small area. It does have some nice brewpubs and good restaurants. There was an opportunity to tour the Coors Brewery also, for me though I went early to the Pepsi Centre, a 15-minute walk from the hotel. They have a great bar/restaurant on site the place to be pre-match. The place is set out like a massive log cabin. Fans were friendly and eager to chat about hockey and their team. On that evening the Leafs were in town and as always there were Toronto shirts in abundance. I spoke to a couple that had driven from Wyoming; it's the only chance they had to see them play live. I had a reasonable seat at the game. Ed Belfour was in goal for the Leafs and he was kept busy, and Milan Hejduk scored a couple of goals assisted by Joe Sakic. Actually this was a great night for me seeing some great players on view like Mats Sundin who scored for the Leafs, but the Avalanche won 5-3 but not before Leafs' hard man and all-round entertainer Tie Domi got involved. He was always in someone's face every time I saw him, the sort of player you buy a ticket to see. The Leafs coach was Pat Quinn who moaned his team were taking too many penalties. Strange fact on the night was that this was the Leafs first visit to Denver since 1997. Not sure why!

My trip finished with a few days in Las Vegas. The flight home was via Phoenix.

During the period 2004–2006 my personal circumstances changed. Firstly my wife and I were divorced and then the company I had worked for 35 years was sold so I took redundancy. It's strange when you are faced with the availability of time (something that I had always been short of) but then needing to balance out the finance. I have since worked in training for a short period of time but was made redundant again so it was time to live the dream and travel without the time restriction, and what a difference the fixture list then reads. Karen and I took a trip to North America at the start of 2007. It did not start in the best circumstances with a flight to Vancouver with British Airways; we had poor seats with arrogant passengers in front. This completely changed our view on international flights and we would in future plan very differently.

There was snow everywhere in Vancouver. It was a lovely scenic view from our hotel (the Pan Pacific). Karen saw her first live NHL game at the GM Place – Canucks v Minnesota Wild. She had been watching ice hockey for a couple of years but not at this level.

Despite the bad weather and a midweek night obtaining tickets for the game was not easy. Ticket exchange/stub-hub did not apply to us it seemed. So as usual I negotiated with touts and managed to get lower level corner seats, a decent view. I waited with anticipation of Karen's view of the NHL standard, arguably the best in the world. I always note the pace of the game, individual speed of thought, stick handling and goal tending. That night one of the best stoppers was in goal for the Canucks, Robert Luongo. I remember seeing him shortly after his move from Florida (his wife was not happy about leaving the Sunshine State). Other great players for the home side included Trevor Linden who as mentioned before was playing in Hastings in 1993, Marcus Naslund and the

Sedin twins (Henrik and Daniel). The game was, though, a fairly low-key affair. The crowd was quiet to start with and then positively silent when Marian Gaborik and Brian Rolston put the Wild 2-0 up in 12 minutes. Only late in the second period did we see any spark from the Canadian side, but that was extinguished with Gaborik's second and Wes Walz scoring the fourth goal to give the Wild a 5-2 win, their first in 11 road games. This game was a sell-out, the Canucks 150th consecutive dating back to 2002 (18,630). Karen needed to see more but it was how quick the game was that stood out for her. After the game you are not short of options for bars/restaurants in the downtown area of Vancouver.

We then took in some winter sun with a four-night trip to Hawaii which is just a beautiful collection of islands. Again there was a flight problem on our internal leg to San Francisco. Our booking had not been confirmed and we only just made the connection. On the return we flew direct to Los Angeles to arrive in plenty of time to see the Anaheim Ducks that evening (my second attempt). But yet again a flight delay left us with a problem. Arriving at Los Angeles Airport at 4.45pm we took the first shuttle bus to Avis car hire and got sorted fairly quickly, but the LA traffic even with six to eight lanes is tough going. The best way is to use the car pool lanes on the freeway and this helped us to get to the Anaheim area by 6.45pm, but then promptly turned the wrong way along East Katella. Eventually after getting to the Honda Centre and parking at a place just over the road, we actually tried to book in the adjacent hotel but it was full. So with luggage left in the car we got to the ticket office at 7.20pm when a strange thing happened. A gentleman walked up and put two tickets in my hand and before I even had chance to ask how much he was gone. So we went in with the tickets and sat down right on 7.30pm next to the very chap who gave me the tickets. He would not accept payment, a drink or anything. They were his company tickets that were not being used that evening. Strange how things turn out after the time I had tickets to the Ducks and never made it.

The Honda Centre is a nice arena just down the road from the Disney complex and only around ten miles from the beach areas. A good selection of bars and restaurants are opposite and a short walk away is the baseball stadium home of the LA Angels. The St Louis Blues were the visitors on that night. The game mirrored the one in Vancouver, a quiet crowd with St Louis taking an early lead. In fact late in the second period that lead had become 5-0, a bad night for the Ducks, but there were a couple of good fights one involving George Parros well known for this side of his game. At least this did get people out of their seats. Eventually though the Blues won 6-2. This proved to be just an off night for Anaheim as we were watching the eventual Stanley Cup Champions crowned later in June 2007. There were some really top players on show for the Ducks that night: Scott and Rob Niedermayer, Chris Pronger, Temmo Selanne, Ryan Getzlaf and Corey Perry.

After the game we had to find a hotel. Anaheim of course is close to the Disney Studios so there is plenty of choice even late at night. We pulled up at a Doubletree Hotel with signs outside advertising rooms at $99, however, once inside they tried to charge us $179. We promptly left. The assistant manager then came out, stopped us and took the car and our luggage and apologised for the error his staff member had made. Now we would only pay $79 and he included a drink at the bar for our inconvenience. So free game tickets, cut-price hotel and even the car hire was a good deal. California couldn't be faulted. We would return.

Actually we caught up with the Ducks again in October 2007 when a pair of regular season games against the Los Angeles Kings started the season in London at the O2 Arena. What a shame these days that our capital city does not have an elite league ice hockey team. The O2 holds around 18,000 and both games on Saturday/Sunday were mostly sold out. Each team had a home game as part of their regular season.

The Stanley Cup was on view, which as mentioned was won by the Ducks just a few months before. Fans of either team travelled from California. I met a Kings fan at the hotel who was ecstatic. He had come over and had taken the train everywhere in the city. It was six hours before the first game but his enthusiasm was unrivalled. The main body of fans came from throughout the UK and mainland Europe but it all lacked atmosphere, the neutrals in the crowd not really supporting either team, so it all seemed a little polite. Even so there was a great deal of talent on show. We were joined by two German fans, Heidi from Frankfurt and Andre from Hannover. They do not get a regular opportunity to see the NHL so they loved the games and friendly banter between different fans from across Europe. I do hope they will consider bringing games here again.

The first game on the Saturday was the Kings home game and they beat the Stanley Cup holders 4-1, Mike Cammalleri with two goals and Jonathan Bernier with 26 saves was making his debut at 19 in the Kings' goal. Bobby Ryan of the Ducks scored to stop the shut out.

The following day's game was just the opposite, this time Anaheim won 4-1, Corey Perry with two goals and a good performance in goal by Swiss National Jonas Hiller. The crowd loved the fight between George Parros (Ducks) and Scott Thornton (Kings); actually Thornton did well against the much bigger Parros. Both games were officially sold out at 17,551 and NHL Commissioner Gary Bettmen commented the facilities were terrific and the hospitality was wonderful.

The NHL came to London many years before the Ducks and Kings faced off at the 02 Arena. Firstly in 1992 Montreal played back-to-back games against the Chicago Blackhawks. These were only pre-season exhibition games played at the Wembley Arena. The teams shared the spoils with a win each. I remember attending the two games played the following year (1993), and again these were pre-season exhibition affairs. The Toronto Maple Leafs lost both games to the New York Rangers 5-3 and 3-1. I recall little about the games. It was a major coup though to bring NHL teams to Britain, a chance to raise the profile of ice hockey in this country was not to be missed.

In 2010 the Belfast Giants organisation deserve much praise for persuading the Boston Bruins to fly over and play a pre-season game. Other players from around the elite league would help boost the Giants squad on the day with the Bruins winning the contest 5-1. I was unable to attend the game but I do support any venture to enhance Great Britain Ice Hockey.

During the early part of 2008 Karen and myself went to New York City. I have been to the Big Apple on two occasions previously but had never experienced any sport there, so a winter trip was called for to view all three of the NHL teams based in the area.

Now regarding the flights, I had long since been in a Star Alliance Air Miles programme, so it was time to use their cash plus miles options following our previous experience. We took a Swiss flight from Birmingham via Zurich in business class. It is the only way to travel. Heavy snow greeted us in New York City. A long cab ride to New Jersey was costly but the Hyatt Hotel was great, also what a terrific view looking over the Hudson River to the famous Manhattan downtown skyline. The transport system was excellent. You can take the subway or ferry. We actually walked from Ground Zero to Times Square seeing the Greenwich Village area and also Canal Street where it seems you can buy anything except nothing is real – Karen bought a Gucci watch! We did walk through one dodgy area, which reminded me caution should always be exercised even if NYC is not like it used to be. Just past Times Square is the Ed Sullivan Theatre. Every day they host the *Late Show With David Letterman* and we put our names down to be in the audience. We were called at our hotel to say we had complimentary reserved seats and the evening was well worth it as we managed to see a very interesting interview with Woody Harrelson.

So on to the first game at the Prudential Centre, home of the New Jersey Devils, an easy subway ride to Newark and it was a short walk through a shopping centre to the arena. We arrived very early so decided to walk into the centre of Newark (not the best move), but the area is to be avoided. We soon went back to the arena, which was a good move because they have a second rink, which was hosting a very entertaining game between the Army and Navy. There were some young players on view and excited parents in the crowd but I really cannot remember who won. The main game was the New Jersey Devils v New York Islanders. It was a good atmosphere with many visiting fans, our seats though were low down and at one end with a couple of kids standing every two seconds making the view awkward, a good game though with the Devils running out 4-2 winners. The scorers were Patrik Elias, John Madden, Zack Parise and Brian Gionta with Martin Brodeur in goal. This was the Devils 47th win of the season on their way to the play-offs.

The following evening was a trip to Madison Square Gardens to see the New York Rangers v Florida Panthers. I had to negotiate tickets from touts (not for the first time). I settled on a painful $100 each actually less than face value. A lesson here though is to be careful what you get yourself into. A rather large gentleman asked me to step into his office to negotiate. I followed him into a subway. There are times in your life when you ask yourself 'what am I doing', and these words were ringing in my ears. Fortunately the chap could not have been nicer. However, think carefully in future I told myself. The seats were behind the goal which was not too bad except for two clowns in front of us who jumped out of their seats every time the Rangers crossed the blue line.

It was an easy win for the Rangers, 5-0, and the Panthers struggled to make an impact against some of the best players in the NHL like goalkeeper Henrik Lundquist and long-time superstar Jaromir Jagr. The evening was an experience as we had been to the New Prudential Stadium a few days before and now we were in the old Madison Square Garden; history aside it's easy to see why teams move to new state of the art facilities.

The last game of the trip was a Monday evening on Long Island to see New York Islanders v Pittsburgh. Now I had already been told where it was and how to get there but I still misjudged it. We should have moved to a hotel near the rink, instead a subway ride from Jersey to Penn Station, Long Island rail to Hampstead Station and then a taxi to the Nassau Coliseum. It was a very wet evening and despite the opposition it was a small crowd. We really liked the arena. It's older but a bit steeper and therefore you have a really good view from the lower level. A strange game this one, the Islanders dominated for long periods and outshot the Penguins 52-21 but still managed to lose the game 4-2. Frustrations boiled over when Mike Comrie (NYI) got involved with a good fight against Tyler Kennedy (Pitt). I could not pick a winner. It was a very enjoyable game overall with the Penguins finishing being the deciding factor.

After the game we quickly got a taxi back to the station. The last train to Manhattan was at 11.05pm.

It was after 1am when we got back to Jersey – another lesson in planning! A good trip though overall.

During October 2008 we embarked on a Midwest trip and it was another rush to a game. I must stop trying to attend games on a long travel day. It started with a BMI flight direct to Chicago arriving around 6pm. A dash through passport control (unusual) and we booked in at an airport Embassy Suites Hotel which is a short shuttle ride. We then took a taxi ($60) to the United Centre and arrived at 7.45pm just enough time to negotiate some tickets. Now it seems the local police are a little more strong minded here about touts in Chicago, so having agreed a really good price for box seats the seller would not take the cash from my hand, instead he insisted I place the money inside page three of a religious newspaper that he seemed to be selling as a front to his touting business, I then handed the paper back. This was not the way I would ever do business but sold out arenas and ticket exchange programmes that did not allow foreign registrations leave you little choice.

The Blackhawks beat Edmonton 3-0 on the night. This was the year the Hawks would go on to win the Stanley Cup with all their young stars – Jonathon Toews, Patrick Kane and Patrick Sharp backed up by Antti Niemi. They already looked the part even at that stage of the season.

The seats were very good with waitress service. The United Centre is an excellent arena with really good viewing areas and there are also small dedicated bars. The location though is just out of the main downtown area and just like the baseball stadiums for the Cubs and White

Sox you should not stray away from the immediate areas. We took a cab back to the airport hotel (another $65).

It was a fairly early start the following day but made easier by being at the airport hotel. A short United Airlines flight for a lunchtime arrival in Pittsburgh, we took the local bus from the airport to the downtown area. It is a cheap option and it works quite well, unfortunately though if you have bags it becomes difficult when the bus starts to fill up. We decided on a taxi back the following day. The hotel was the Omni William Penn, it dates back to 1916 and it is quite superb. The exterior dominates the downtown skyline and inside it is elegant and stylish. People were gathering for afternoon tea and I almost forgot we were there for ice hockey. The Pittsburgh Penguins play at the Mellon arena so called the 'Igloo' due to its shape. It's just a ten-minute walk from the hotel uphill to the 'Mario Lemieux Place' named after their legendary player. It's tough to get tickets but I managed to buy two from a gentleman at face value, centre ice, lower level, a top view.

The visitors were the Carolina Hurricanes and the game started with a fight between Paul Bissonette (Pits) and Dan LaCouture (Car), I say a fight it was more like an assault by Bissonette. The Canes then took the lead with a first ever NHL goal by Brandon Sutter (19 at the time). The crowd seem to be waiting for the Penguin big guns to fire, and finally in the third period they did scoring four unanswered goals, two inside 32 seconds, Sidney Crosby and Evgeni Malkin were both on the scoresheet in a 4-1 win. It was a good entertaining night. I like Pittsburgh as a city, it is of course a steel city, but it is also known as a city of bridges. It has even more bridges than Venice apparently, also there are three rivers that run through it, Allegheny, Monongahela and Ohio.

The following day we flew to St Louis. We caught a train downtown (not bag friendly) to Union Station. The Fairmont Hotel was a short walk from the Mississippi River which runs right along the city with river cruises and casinos to choose from. The famous arch is the main St Louis landmark. We viewed all of this with a walk to the Blues Stadium, and it takes you right past Busch Stadium, home of the St Louis Cardinals. There are some good pubs/restaurants in the area for pre-game entertainment. I again paid touts for tickets – not bad seats for the game against the Los Angeles Kings and Sarah Palin and her children made the puck drop on this night.

A capacity crowd (19,150) saw the Kings goaltender on the night be the deciding factor, shutting out the Blues to help the Kings win 4-0. Actually St Louis only had 15 shots on goal but Jason Labarbera, known more for his back up roll made vital stops during Blues pressure on four power play opportunities. Playing on the night for St Louis was Paul Kariya who had played the best part of his career for the Ducks (nine seasons). I had seen him playing for Canada in Bolzano (Italy) in 1994 during his early career, a really top player.

The next flight was to Texas for a weekend in Dallas. On the bus ride downtown from the airport you pass the old Cowboys' Stadium. You just can't help thinking back to JR and the Southfork Ranch.

The arena was an easy walk from the hotel. Touts are

again the order of the day. I was now getting experienced in negotiating. Outside there were bars, restaurants and a band playing – it was a lively Saturday night and a good atmosphere. The game was against the Washington Capitals. If it's goals you want this was the night to visit Dallas, 11 in total, with the Capitals winning in overtime. There were some top players on the scoresheet during the game; for the Stars, Sean Avery (a controversial figure who had many problems during his 12-year NHL career) and Mike Modano, who moved to Dallas with the North Stars when they folded in Minnesota. He even had a small part in one of the *Mighty Ducks* films alongside fellow player Basil McRae. Modano has now retired after 21 NHL seasons. For all but one (Detroit) he played for the North Stars Franchise and was part of the Dallas Stanley Cup winning team in 1999. For the Capitals two goals for Sergei Fedorov and the overtime winner from Alexander Semin. There was even a fight involving Donald Brashear (Caps) v Krys Barch (Dal).

The following day was a chance to take in the sights – the area where JFK was shot looks like a normal building and it's hard to picture what happened. We managed a nice Texas steak in the evening.

Our next destination was Los Angeles; our hotel was within walking distance of the Staples Centre and all the LA live entertainment. The game was the Kings v Detroit Red Wings. I paused for a photograph outside the arena next to the Wayne Gretzky statue (ok I know, I have done this before). Our seats were behind the goal only two rows from the front, a really good view for the most part, except the far end goal and trying to see through the players on the ice was difficult. Even so, I do like to be close to the action. There were hundreds of Red Wing fans at the game and they even threw a rubber octopus on the ice in the third period. This is a tradition at their home games it seems. The game was fairly even and ended 3-3 following a Detroit equaliser by Valtteri Filppula at 18.06 in the third period. The Red Wings then won the shootout 2-0 with goals from their main men, Pavel Datsyuk and Henrik Zetterberg.

The following day we took a four-hour drive north towards San Francisco as we head to San Jose. You seem to be driving for ever just to get out of Los Angeles. We had a satnav with the car and it worked taking us straight to the door of the Fairmont Hotel. It is a classy hotel, well positioned for the town and walking distance to the HP Pavilion, home of the Sharks. On route there is an English style pub which is obviously a pre-match drinking place for the fans. The bar it seemed was once owned by Owen Nolan (ex-Sharks) so we were informed. Tickets were not so easy to obtain there, we were assured extra seats would be released before the start, but I am not sure they meant that particular game. Pittsburgh Penguins were the visitors which is always an added attraction. In the end I paid a tout for two tickets (only face value), not bad seats, corner view, first tier, around $85 dollars each.

The Penguins were disappointing and the Sharks defence kept Sidney Crosby and Evgeni Malkin scoreless although they did get an assist on their only goal of the night late in the third period. Joe Pavelski and Mike Grier scored the Sharks goals in a 2-1 win. The Sharks goalkeeper was Evgeni Nabokov who only faced 11 shots on his goal; playing in defence for San Jose was Rob Blake who always looked class whenever I saw him during his career.

It was a much longer drive for our final stop of the trip in Phoenix. The arena in Glendale is really impressive as mentioned previously though the location is an issue. We stayed at the hotel on the complex; shopping, bars and restaurants were in abundance. After the game there are cinemas and bowling if you wish. We started with a few drinks at the Yard House; it has a massive choice of beers and wines from around the world. You can just walk up and buy your choice of ticket prior to the game. On this occasion they were giving out free white T-shirts to attempt a 'white-out' at the game. The visitors were the Minnesota Wild who edged the game 3-2. Olli Jokinen scored both Coyotes goals, the game was a little tame with very few penalties, Wayne Gretzky was the Phoenix coach at that time. The attendance at the Jobing.com arena was 14,817 and it had been an enjoyable evening to finish the trip especially as Arizona is one of my favourite states in the USA.

The next trip was over a Christmas and New Year period in 2009/10. This was the first time that I had managed this due to my work commitments. We flew to Los Angeles and on to Las Vegas on Christmas Eve and spent four nights. It felt extremely festive there. After a lovely few days we then flew back east to Washington DC. It really is a long ride downtown from the airport (why is this the case in North America?). We stayed opposite the Verizon

Centre – home of the Capitals. It was a comfortable hotel – a former post office – but boy was it cold. I complained so many times about the room, the manager kept giving us free breakfasts, drinks, you name it.

We managed to get some tickets again from touts. It was a game against the Carolina Hurricanes. Now I often talk about atmosphere in the NHL (or lack of it). That night was very good. Also I think just everyone there wears a red or white Caps shirt most with Ovechkin on the back. On the night though, despite his speed and Caps dominance, it was a smash and grab raid by the Hurricanes, Cam Ward being the main villain of the peace. The crowd was stunned when the Carolina Hurricanes took a first period 3-0 lead and despite coming back in the third period to 3-4 the Canes ran out 6-3 winners, Eric Staal with two goals and Cam Ward facing 31 shots. A full house of over 18,000 saw the game.

The cold in January in Washington DC can seriously damage your ears. A decision to do a walking tour of the city was excellent, seeing the White House, Capitol Building and the J E Hoover Building was not to be missed. However, you need to wear the right clothes including earmuffs. It was such a beautiful sunny day that we were totally deceived (it's all down to the wind chill factor). Our second match in Washington lead us back to the Verizon Centre. Too cold to walk around, we purchased two tickets at $50 each to watch my first and only NBA game, the Washington Wizards v Oklahoma Thunder; basketball is not a game I have ever followed except to dip in and out of on TV. I do remember Michael Jordan and Dennis Rodman of the Chicago

Bulls winning many titles, the game though seems to be end to end until the last throws which seems to decide the match, all a bit stop/start for me. On the night though I thought we would watch a couple of quarters and then go for a meal, but with great seats, and a good game, we stayed right until the end. Oklahoma Thunder won the game with one of their NBA superstars on show (Kevin Durant). What a good evening's entertainment it turned out to be.

The next day was a taxi to Union Station, a splendid historical building made even more attractive with the festive decorations. We caught an Amtrak Train to Raleigh, North Carolina. The ride took us through Quantico where the headquarters of the FBI are.

We spent New Year's Eve in Raleigh. It's only a small place with a little history; the game on New Year's Eve was against the New York Rangers. We had already booked tickets. Now this is a typical situation in the US. You ask how to get to the arena and they expect everyone will drive. Public Transport – what, out there? You must be joking! It was a taxi we ended up using ($60). The arena is situated off the main drag well out of town. It left us a little concerned on getting a taxi back being New Year's Eve.

All fans attending the game were given free entry to a suite area after the game where the club had arranged a bar, live band and a buffet – very nice too. We left a little before midnight but had to wait a while for a taxi. The club officials were very helpful and called one for us. Earlier in the evening we were surprised at the level of security at the arena. It was an airport style entry, quite strict, which is why it was surprising they only opened 45 minutes prior to the face off. The game was played at a good pace, both teams going for the win. Tom Kostopoulos (Car) fought Aaron Voros (NYR) in the second period, a good battle in keeping with the game. It was through Brandon Dubinsky (NYR) assisted by Marian Gaborik that sealed the 2-1 win for New York. The referee (Dan O'Halloran) did leave under a cloud though when he ruled out a Brandon Sutter goal for Carolina on review during the second period. He did not leave with Happy New Year ringing in his ears. There were 17,000 fans in attendance at the game. I really did like the arena in Raleigh.

On New Year's Day we walked all around the centre part of Raleigh. It's only a small downtown area but quite pleasant. People seemed very friendly. Late afternoon we boarded a flight to Tampa, collected a car and drove to the downtown Embassy Suites, a perfect location for the Lightning Arena (five minutes' walk). As always with downtown hotels they charge an arm and a leg to park.

The deal we took included a match ticket for the following day. You do not get a choice of seat though and we were behind the goal but it was a good view. The game was against the Penguins who had a huge contingent of fans but not many actually from Pittsburgh I would guess. It was a 3pm start so outside in 70-degree weather there were food stalls, bars and a live band. It was there we met two fans from the Hull Stingrays on holiday in Florida. The arena was excellent inside with wide concourses where everyone eats and drinks. I would love to know what the takings were on that day! The game belonged to Martin St Louis. Although in his thirties now, the Penguins could not handle him; speed and skill in abundance, it was indeed St Louis who scored first for Tampa Bay with a backhand shot close in after just one minute of the game. The Lightning would go on to win 3-1 and not for the first time for me the Penguins had failed to impress.

The following day we drove south to see the Florida Panthers. It's around four hours. The arena is miles from Miami just like the Marlins (MLB). However, now they have a new arena near Miami and have changed their name. This was due to very poor crowds. The Panthers do not have massive support either. On route we got lost somehow so I asked at a hotel near Fort Lauderdale who printed me directions – no problem. We followed them to the letter and ended up at a high school and one turning later had us being watched from all corners. We were in a very bad area. We drove away at speed. It took us a little while to calm down. The time was then 3.30pm (game was at 5pm). I stopped at a bike shop (it looked busy). Inside it was full of Hell's Angels. Everyone turned around and when I spoke I felt all of Miami was looking at me. But the shop people could not have been more helpful. Sunrise was the area we needed to get to and it was five miles further than the directions had shown.

We found a hotel near the arena. One of the staff drove us to the entrance. We collected our tickets and on walking into the club shop we met two lovely ladies from the Coventry Blaze who gave me a huge hug. This was turning out to be a strange day. The visitors were again the Penguins. I would imagine their VIP travel arrangements would not have encountered our difficulties. Not so many fans this time with Penguin (Crosby) shirts. In fact the arena looked only half full. Perhaps fans had been studying the same map we did. My jinx on the Penguins continued as this time they take a two goal lead in the first period including a wrist shot from Crosby, but then the Panthers hit six unanswered goals including a hat trick from Radek Dvorak to complete a 6-2 win. There were only four minor penalties in the game and the official attendance was over 18,000, but it did not look like half that number.

We ended the day with a welcome meal back at the hotel with a few stiff drinks. We drove back to Tampa for the flight home the following day.

The year 2011 became a really massive year in more ways than one. During the early part of the year I put together a trip to allow me to complete my visits to all the NHL arenas. We started by taking the daily Air New Zealand flight to Los Angeles using our air miles and cash to allow us to travel in business class. We used the lounge facilities at London Heathrow before the flight. The service on board was top class. On arrival we caught an onward Southwest internal flight to Las Vegas and stayed at the new 'City Centre' resort, The Vdara. It is excellent and well recommended.

After a few days relaxing we took a Delta flight to Atlanta. It was a train ride downtown to the CNN complex. Unfortunately it is not a rail system designed for carrying a bag or two. Our hotel was in the complex. It was easy to purchase a ticket for the Atlanta Thrashers.

There is an excellent sports bar next to CNN and rumours were circulating that there would not be an NHL team in Atlanta the following season. We missed the opportunity to tour the CNN building to concentrate on the evening game against the Florida Panthers. Both teams were probably out of the play-off race but still it was a very exciting game.

Each team traded goals leaving the game level at 3-3 at the end of regulation. Blake Wheeler then scored the winner for the Thrashers 25 seconds into overtime (his second of the night). I thought this was a top game with goals, a good fight and some impressive displays on the night from Andrew Ladd, Evander Kane and Dustin Byfuglien for Atlanta, and Thomas Vokoun in goal for Florida facing 36 shots. The arena was excellent: good views, great location, it's a shame there will no longer be NHL games played there.

The following day we decided on a taxi to the airport. It was another Delta flight this time to Minneapolis St Paul arriving at midday. Snow was all around and temperatures were minus ten degrees. We took a taxi to the Hilton in the downtown area. St Paul provides skywalks from building to building so we walked to the arena indoors. We purchased lower level centre ice tickets for the 5pm game against the Buffalo Sabres who brought more than a few fans with them. The bar across the street was a typical mid-western bar with ice hockey memorabilia posted everywhere. The game was sold out. The Minnesota Wild are a fairly new team but fans still remember the North Stars moving to Dallas.

The arena is excellent with wide concourses, good

viewing and a lively crowd. They have certain stalls there that sell every dessert that's bad for you. We settled on crepes with chocolate and ice cream, not very hockey like but once you see it you have to have it. We are stopped at the interval for a chat by an ex-Nottingham Panther, Eric Nelson and his wife, who were in the area. They recognised my shirt – a nice couple that speak fondly of Nottingham. A shame we had little time with the game re-starting. The game itself was a tight affair with Buffalo taking an early lead through Rob Niedermayer. However, during the second period the Wild hit back to level the game at 2-2. The Sabres would go on to win it in overtime with a goal from Drew Stafford. In all it had been a very enjoyable afternoon.

The following day we had a relaxing day in St Paul and had a chance to visit the largest shopping mall in the United States. It was more than an interesting bus ride out there with some eccentric locals making us smile. It is a massive mall, which is well worth a visit.

Our next flight was on United Airlines at lunchtime which put us in Philadelphia in mid-afternoon. Now it was a dilemma where to stay because the arena is between the airport and downtown and we had just 18 hours there. Eventually we decided to stay at the Hilton Airport Hotel. It was a taxi (four miles) to and from the arena which is next to the baseball and football stadiums. There was nothing in the area pre-match, but there were plenty of food/drink bar areas in the arena. We had seats in the middle section (second tier) front row. It was a good view on the blue line. The game was the Philadelphia Flyers against Edmonton Oilers; the Alberta team had no chance of making the play-offs and had a fairly young side at that time, so it was a learning curve for some of the team. Frankly though they were poor on the night. Chris Pronger and the Philly defence may well never have such an easy night. The Flyers went on to win the game comfortably 4-1 with two goals from Jeff Carter.

The next day was an easy check-in and a US Air flight to Detroit where we picked up a car and headed downtown to the MGM Casino Hotel. The Red Wings have a great NHL history. I had wanted to visit the Joe Louis arena for many years. My first thoughts on the city was it seemed old and run down. We could see the arena from the hotel but were advised not to walk, so a taxi was called. The doors did not open until one hour prior to the game and a massive queue formed which snaked through a run-down car park. The back of the arena looks across the river at Windsor inside the Canadian border. Inside it felt like we were back in time. There was only one concourse. It's all the same level. To enter the seat areas you go through velvet curtains like entering a theatre. We were close to the back so the climb to our seats required a certain level of fitness. It also meant fans were moving in and out in front of you all night.

The game was against the LA Kings. The Detroit side sounded like an all-star team when it was announced. Names like Nicklas Lidstrom, Pavel Datsyuk, Henrik Zetterberg, Todd Bertuzzi, Johan Franzen and Mike Modano, it's hardly surprising that over 20,000 fans flock to every game. Retired shirts ring the arena including 'Hall of Fame' Steve Yzerman. On that night though the Red Wings were up against a resilient Los Angeles Kings side that despite being under pressure for long periods stole the game 2-1 with Slovenian, Anze Kopitar, on the scoresheet. My night was complete when the Red Wings veteran announcer (I believe this to have been Budd Lynch) was showing a group of fans his Stanley Cup Ring. I had a good close-up of this and it really added to the whole experience.

We stayed an extra night in Detroit so decided we would walk around the city. We were informed it was a city with a previous bad reputation trying to re-build itself. The locals seemed proud. We visited the Detroit Tigers stadium and covered quite a good part of downtown.

The following day (Friday) the weather stayed cold but no real snow, which made our drive to Columbus fairly easy (around four hours). We stayed at the Hyatt, which is within touching distance of the arena. It's the opposite of the Joe Louis; modern with plenty of food and drinks establishments in the complex next door with happy hour and live entertainment. Our seats were lower level in one corner but still a decent view.

The Los Angeles Kings were again the visitors and it was that man, Anze Kopitar, again, this time with a hat trick on the night. In fact the Blue Jackets were outplayed by the Kings for long periods. Even so, Jonathan Bernier (in goal in place of Jonathan Quick) still had to face 34 shots. Rick Nash one of Columbus's main men disappointed on the night and the Kings sealed the game with a Justin Williams goal at 58.26 which resulted in a mass exodus. It was to be expected but unfortunately a gentleman in front decided on his way to leave that he would stand in front of everyone and hold a lengthy conversation. He then took exception when being told to take his seat. No stewards were in the area and it could have turned nasty. We have experienced this with fans in North America before. However, this incident must not cloud our view of the Blue Jacket organisation. We enjoyed our evening.

It was an early start to leave at 7.30am the following morning; it was a four-hour drive and a return to Pittsburgh to visit the new arena. We had booked to stay at the Doubletree Hotel. The game was a 2pm start against the Montreal Canadiens, and it was a five-minute walk to the arena from the hotel.

What a beautiful, crisp and sunny day it was in Pittsburgh but our plans were derailed when we sat in traffic for over an hour due to a St Patrick's Day parade. We booked in and rushed to the box office. The game was sold out and despite my attempts through e-mails and phone calls we failed to get tickets. We were, though, assured the box office would find us tickets and they did. There was a choice of right on the back row (nose bleed level) or top seats centre ice with private bar and food areas ($200 each). Just let's say we have more money than sense. We did not regret it – a great afternoon. Not so for the Penguins though with their team being shut out by Carey Price in a 3-0 Montreal win. In truth, Pittsburgh never got going in this matinee game. Attendance was 18,310, which was the clubs 200th consecutive sell-out spanning the two arenas. On this day the fans spent most of the time booing and whistling P K Subban (Montreal defenceman) who I was assured had been the villain of the piece in previous games. It did not put him off. Actually I think he hits as hard as anyone in the NHL.

On Sunday morning we left Pittsburgh in different conditions – it was snowing and it was another four-hour drive. (It's always four hours it seems.) This journey would be a return to Buffalo, New York. After all these years we were joined at the Adams Mark Hotel by my friend (Gerrie) who had crossed the border from Stoney Creek. We had indeed attended the game in Buffalo at the Auditorium over 20 years ago.

We walked to the arena. I don't think Buffalo would look right even if it was not cold and dreary. Our seats were up high in the third tier but it was still a decent view. The Sabres' fans unfurled a football like flag behind the goal – it looked impressive. The team had a real chance of the play-offs so the crowd was up for the game. Ottawa were the visitors who stayed with Buffalo throughout the game. Jason Spezza scored two goals, but the Sabres were always the better side and went on to win 6-4 with Austrian Thomas Vanek getting one of the goals, and he was constant danger to the Senators throughout the game. We struggled after the game to find a decent bar/ restaurant so the hotel had to do.

The next day was a drive across the border into Canada, a much easier transition than I recall years before. We stopped at Niagara Falls, parts of which were still frozen – a fascinating sight! Next it was lunch at Tim Horton's. It just feels right to go there. It was then on to Toronto (via Gerrie's satnav). We stayed at the Radisson on Harbourfront, an excellent choice. We had a pre-match meal on Front Street before we went on to the Air Canada Centre. It's strange I did not notice any touts that evening. I usually had a date with them. Perhaps it was because Canadian friends had purchased tickets for us as a gift for the evening game. How very kind.

This was my second visit to the centre and you cannot fault the facilities. The Leafs' fans were in good voice and there was still a chance of the play-offs. Tampa Bay Lightning were the visitors and proved far too good for the Leafs on the night. The Bolts had Martin St Louis and Steve Stamkos threatening throughout with long-time star Vincent LeCavalier scoring a second period goal in a 6-2 win. Toronto had plenty of effort posting 32 shots on veteran Dwayne Roloson, but Phil Kessel and the rest of the Leafs came up short. I really enjoyed the contest; it is always a thrill to be in Toronto at a game.

The final leg of the trip for me to complete my visits to all the NHL arenas would see us head to Ottawa. Guess what? It's around a four-hour drive. Actually we had been very lucky with the weather and it was really nice sunny day although there had obviously been much snow in Ottawa. We stayed at the Chateau Laurier, an imposing hotel overlooking the city. The arena is quite a distance out of town but there are buses to the game from 6pm. However, when several buses arrived already full we decided not to take a chance of arriving late so we went back for the car. It takes at least 45 minutes to get there and the car park was a mudbath following the melted snow. We caught up again with the Pittsburgh Penguins who were the visitors. The game was one sided and, for a change, this time the Penguins outplayed their opponents, Tyler Kennedy and Jordan Staal scored the goals in a 5-1 impressive win. The Senators fans tried to rally their team but this would not be their night.

We celebrated back at the hotel on my completion of the NHL – 36 arenas have taken me over 20 years. A glass of champagne was called for with a slice of cheesecake – what else!

The following day we took a direct flight home with Air Canada. Some things though, even many years on, do not change and I again started to feel dreadful. It was a cold, then flu with a chest infection and steroids were required. Not the best way to end a trip.

Within weeks of my return, the NHL announced the Atlanta Thrashers were no more and the franchise would move to Winnipeg. The Jets would be back after 15 years even if it was by a strange route. For me though I would need to go there, of course, otherwise my complete NHL list would not be valid.

During October 2011 the NHL returned to Europe with several regular season games in Helsinki, Stockholm and Berlin. Karen's favourite team is the Los Angeles Kings so we headed to Stockholm to see the game against the New York Rangers and on to Berlin for a game there against the Buffalo Sabres.

Stockholm's Globe Arena is a much older building than Hartwell (Helsinki) and the O2 (Berlin). Our view was behind the goal and not the best. New York Rangers fans far outnumbered the Kings and there were many fans there from across Europe. It still did not look sold out though and perhaps the high ticket prices (£95 each) and the extravagant costs of just about everything in Stockholm may have prevented some fans from attending.

The game started slow, almost pedestrian-like, until halfway through the first period when Anze Kopitar scored with a great slapshot. Ryan Callaghan equalised for the Rangers though at 15.22. There was no scoring in the second period but a fight broke out between Kyle Clifford (LA) and Brandon Prust (NYR). In the third period Marian Gaborik put New York ahead but Mike Richards sent the game into overtime with a tip in at 55.01. Ryan McDonagh was called for tripping in overtime and the King's defenceman, Jack Johnson, stepped into the play and forced home the winner with 52 seconds left. Two of the world's best goalkeepers were on view on the night, Henrik Lundquist (NYR) and Jonathan Quick (LA).

We had the pleasure of meeting some LA Kings' fans who were taking a tour of Northern Europe in addition to seeing the Kings. We also met some charming people who worked for the NHL Players' Association. I took the opportunity to bore them with my considered view of ticket prices, problems getting tickets (exchange programmes) and ESPN losing the rights to cover NHL games. They were so nice though and showed a great amount of patience listening to my rant (I did apologise!).

While in Stockholm we took a side trip to Linkoping (around two hours by train). Now if you ever think British Rail has a difficult pricing structure well Swedish Rail advised us to travel first class because the tickets would be 200 krona per person cheaper than in second class. Ten minutes' walk from the station is the Linkoping Arena; they play in the 'A' league in Sweden. Tickets for a seat on the side (a really good view) cost £28. The arena was reasonable although prices were just as expensive for food and drink as Stockholm. The game featured the then current league leaders the Frolunda Indians from Gothenburg. It was an excellent game played at a high standard. The home team won 2-1 and it was a very enjoyable game. The last train back was 10pm so we were pleased it did not go to overtime.

The following day the flight to Berlin was full of Los Angeles media. It was very interesting to listen to conversations. It was a good start because the Express train to the airport is 2 for 1 on a Saturday that made it seem like an ordinary fare. We arrived at Tegel airport and caught a train to Friedrichstr station. We were staying at the Eurostars Hotel tucked away off the main area. It was quiet and it was made even better when we were upgraded to a suite. This would have made even the LA media jealous. We like Berlin and try to walk everywhere. It's 2.8 miles to the O2 arena so a pleasant late Saturday afternoon stroll was called for. The O2 is in the old east part of Berlin and just a short walk from Berlin Ost station. There is a strange mix of old and new buildings along the way. The old arena where the Berlin Eisebarens used to play was not far from the new building.

The game was the LA Kings v Buffalo Sabres. The Sabres had big support on the night swelled by many Austrians there to see Thomas Vanek with the locals cheering for Christian Erhoff, the German defenceman who had just joined them from Vancouver. Standing sections at each end provided a good atmosphere although nothing like a Berlin game. Beating the New York Rangers did not provide any momentum for the

Kings in this game, in fact they looked rather flat and by the middle of the second period the Sabres had built up a three-goal lead including a brace from Luke Adam. The Kings did wake up with two goals from Kopitar but Buffalo were easy 4-2 winners with their keeper Ryan Miller making 31 saves.

Our final trip of the year was during November 2011; this would see us incorporate the Winnipeg Jets. Again this would bring me right up to date with the NHL and take my total to 37.

We started though with some sunshine and an Air New Zealand flight on Thursday, 24th November to Los Angeles where we picked up a car and drove to Huntington Beach for a couple of nights. The Waterfront Hotel is right over from the beach. Friday was a holiday in the States; we started with a walk on the beach and breakfast outside. It was a shorts day as 75 degrees was just perfect weather. We then headed to Anaheim (15 miles). We of course know the arena and where to park. It was a 1.05pm start against the Chicago Blackhawks. It was just a little after 11am but the bars across the street were in full swing. There were plenty of Blackhawks fans in town. The last season we watched Chicago they went on to win the Stanley Cup. Things have changed a little since then. Our seats on the day were perfect – second tier, second row, centre ice. What a matinee game this turned out to be! The Ducks jumped into a 2-0 lead, in fact by the second period they led 4-2, Teemu Selanne on the scoresheet for the home side. However, despite the early dominance, it was the

Blackhawks that hit back and squeezed out a 6-5 win thanks to a Patrick Sharp hat trick and a brace from Jonathan Toews. Chicago had 42 shots on goal and in the end just about deserved the points.

On to Saturday (80 degrees), after a venture on to the Pier it was a 20-mile drive to downtown LA. Getting to our hotel, the Ritz Carlton, next to the Staples Centre, required several trips around the block – a local car show was causing some traffic disruption. The hotel is a perfect location for all the LA live entertainment. We relaxed at the rooftop pool, which has great views of the area. The Blackhawks were following us and were the visitors that evening to the Staples Centre. Before the game Sean joined us for a drink at the Yard house. He is a Kings season ticket holder who we met in Stockholm. It's always good to get an insight on the Kings and NHL in general. His thoughts actually mirrored ours in the fact that the Kings seemed to lack a bit of passion. Sean also felt Dustin Penner was not having enough impact – when he was fit that is. The game though was just another win for the Blackhawks. This time, however, it was a tight game with very few penalty minutes. Defences were on top, Duncan Keith (Chi) and Drew Doughty (LA) both logged more than 25 minutes of ice time. It is goals of course that win matches though and it was Toews again for the Blackhawks with the winner in front of a crowd of 18,118 at the Staples Centre.

On Sunday we headed to Las Vegas. It was a four to five-hour drive. We stayed at the Encore Hotel (part of the Wynn Corporation). On this visit we had no ice hockey, so instead the following day Karen and myself got married. Having been collected at our hotel, we were taken on a short drive in a stretch limo to one of the many small chapels. You just had to smile when the preacher arrived. Wearing a cream suit I thought we were in a scene from *Randall and Hopkirk (Deceased),* and he also had this southern accent with every word rolling on and on. It was just a great experience, a nice, simple ceremony. It was such a lovely day.

We resumed with our tour on Wednesday, 30th November with a flight to Denver. Again, I complained about the distance from the airport. We took a taxi ($60). The Adams Hotel is now the Sheraton and it's my third stay at this hotel. It's more for the location really. It was Karen's first visit to Denver so we did quite a bit of walking in the main area before going over to the Pepsi Centre for the game. The New Jersey Devils were in Denver that evening, but quite frankly they provided little opposition as the Avalanche scored three goals on their first five shots on Martin Brodeur's goal. Ilya Kovalchuk reduced the arrears for the Devils but Colorado went on to win 6-1 with six different scorers on the night.

The following morning the visibility was very poor; mist and snow dominated the skyline – it was suddenly winter as we left for the airport. There were not many choices on that day for NHL games. We took a Southwest flight to San Jose where at least the weather would be 75 degrees. Unfortunately though we ran into the Santa Ana winds and got thrown all over the place on the flight. The landing was some experience. We really did begin to question our decision to go to San Jose. Again we stayed at the Fairmont Hotel downtown, where opposite was a quaint German Christmas market. It felt odd as the weather was 80 degrees and wall-to-wall sun, but it was 1st December. Montreal Canadiens were the visitors to Northern California in the evening. There were only two minor penalties in the whole game. The Habs led three times until Ryane Clowe tied the contest at 58.34 for the Sharks. The game was so tight it went to overtime and then to six rounds of penalty shots until Joe Pavelski got one past Carey Price for a Sharks winner.

Friday, 2nd December, it was destination Winnipeg. Our flight was via Denver where we connected on to Air Canada. We arrived late in the evening and took a taxi downtown to the Place Louis Hotel. Over the road is a Boston Pizza bar/restaurant. It was minus ten degrees and you certainly knew it. Good bar though with split screens showing plenty of hockey.

The following day was a walking tour of Winnipeg with ears and hands well covered. Hot chocolate at the market was the order of the day except they seemed to empty the sugar bowl into it. The town reminds me a little of Hamilton but seems smaller. The Jets arena, the MTS Centre, is downtown and an easy walk. A visit to the Jets shop took up a couple of hours due to how packed it was. The team's return has been a big hit. We set out early for the game having been warned that every bar and restaurant would be full by 5pm – and so it proved to be. We squeezed in and had wings at a bar in what seemed like an English style pub. On to the arena which is a little smaller than most but has a great atmosphere. We had top seats 'centre ice'. It seemed strange though having the previous season seen the Thrashers play in Atlanta and of course most of the players were on that team. I guess that's just sport where finance dictates. In an ideal world the Jets would never have left in the first place. It was those New Jersey Devils that were in town and this time they provided a much better opponent. In fact by the middle of the second period Patrick Elias had put them 2-1 ahead. However, an enthusiastic home crowd were on their feet to applaud a double from Evander Kane to seal the points in a 4-2 win. A capacity crowd of 15,004 were in attendance.

So on this night I completed the NHL again (for now!). It seems though New York City (Brooklyn) will call in 2015/16 when the New York Islanders move there.

We left Winnipeg on an early morning flight (actually delayed). This put us in Calgary just after lunch. Heavy snow greeted us but fortunately I had booked a car with snow tyres. We drove to Banff which needed to be slow and careful. It was like a winter wonderland – a real Christmas feel about the place especially at the Banff Springs Hotel where we stayed. Wildlife seemed to wander freely everywhere especially near the hotel. On our return from an evening meal in the downtown area we walked within a few feet of a rather large Moose just munching away on some hanging tree leaves, just a great sight!

It was a little easier driving back to Calgary. We stayed central at the Place Rou Hotel where a nice log fire greeted us in reception. It was an easy walk or tram ride to the Saddledome for the evening's game against the Carolina Hurricanes. We arrived early to get a seat in the bar/restaurant at the arena. Our seats that evening were in the second tier/blue line. The game was a total shoot out involving 13 goals; the Flames started well and jumped into a three-goal lead in the opening period and late in the third after exchanging goal after goal they led 6-4. The Canes removed their goalie and promptly conceded a seventh. They continued without a keeper in the final minute and scored twice in a frantic finale but went down 7-6. Iginla (Cal) and Staal (Car) both scored twice; there was even a penalty shot scored by Jiri Tlusty (Car) against the Flames keeper Miika Kiprusoff. A large midweek crowd of around 20,000 saw the game.

The following day was the final leg of our trip. We drove up to Edmonton, which is 190 miles. There was snow around and the crosswinds made it another difficult drive. We stopped for petrol and my hands felt numb; should have put the gloves on. We stayed downtown at the Fairmont. Valet parking though turned out to be abandon your car time.

Rexall Place is several stops on a local train. Unfortunately the bar/restaurant I had visited next to the arena some years before was no longer there. In fact the arena is looking tired these days and in need of refurbishment. Perhaps I am being a little harsh and maybe my thinking is swayed with some of the new state of the art venues.

The Carolina Hurricanes made the same trip north with us. They again hit the goal trail in the game this time running out 5-3 winners. A rising star for the Canes is Jeff Skinner with one of the goals. This was the fourth time I have seen him and in my opinion he is definitely one of the NHL stars of the future. A major fight in the third period between Andy Sutton (Edm) and Tim Gleason (Car) got the crowd of 16,839 going but Gleason ended up being thrown out of the game.

It was the end of the trip. We went back to the bar at the Fairmont where a couple of lovely locals bought us a cocktail. The bartender informed us she felt colder in England than Alberta. Interesting comment. For us, well, it started in California sunny and in the 80s, it finished in Alberta at minus ten. In between we saw seven games and 55 goals, we got married in Vegas and I again completed the NHL in Winnipeg. Not sure what to plan next! The following day we dropped off the hire car which now looked like a sheet of ice, We then took a direct Air Canada flight home. It had certainly been an adventure!

At the end of that season (June 2012) the LA Kings would go on to win the Stanley Cup. It just shows how a team develops throughout the season; make a couple of trades (Jack Johnson was a surprise) and go on to conquer all.

The following season 2012/13 there was another lockout in the NHL and fans around the world were baffled. The best league in the world with a $4.2 billion turnover is on strike. There are of course many reasons why agreements need to be reached and both sides were working tirelessly to sort it out. However, it paints the sport in a poor light. Eventually things did get finalised and a shortened programme got underway but not until late January 2013. The Chicago Blackhawks won the Stanley Cup in game six against the Boston Bruins in the final.

A full NHL season would see a return in 2013/14. We would only make it to one game in the whole season though. In March 2014 we visited Indian Wells, California to see the APT Tennis event and made a side trip to Anaheim to see a Monday night game against the Toronto Maple Leafs. There were Leafs fans everywhere and they were not to be disappointed when their team won a hard fought game 3-1, Phil Kessel with one of the goals and the Leafs stopper Jonathan Bernier with 43 saves. There were three fights during the game to keep the fans on their feet. It was well worth the trip to see the game.

It was again the Los Angeles Kings that would go on to win the Stanley Cup, their second in just three seasons, this time in dramatic fashion winning the series against the Sharks, Ducks and Blackhawks all in game seven. They even came back from three games down against the Sharks. New York Rangers provided the opposition for the final and this time the Kings would take only five games to secure the cup. Los Angeles are a strong side and again they added to their squad at the right time (Marian Gaborik), but it was those players who do not always get the headlines that made a massive difference to the Kings like Matt Green, Willie Mitchell, Justin Williams and perhaps a future star, Tyler Toffoli. The Kings will be difficult to beat in the coming years with the challenge I feel mainly coming from Chicago and perhaps Anaheim (just my opinion of course).

Our next venture would not be until March 2015. Unfortunately Karen had to undergo major back surgery in 2014 and was therefore unable to travel.

We took a late afternoon British Airways flight to Montreal on Thursday 19th March. The trip got off to a great start when we were upgraded to first class; top seats and top service. It's surely the only way to travel.

Snow was everywhere in Montreal when we arrived. It was cold but fresh at minus five. The following day we embarked on a walking tour of the city; covering your ears is a must. There are several lovely cathedrals, museums and art galleries amongst many splendid old buildings which are surrounded by skyscrapers. Many people there live in downtown apartments or townhouses and snow was piled higher than some of their windows. This was Quebec! Saturday was game day and after 15 years I returned to the Bell Centre. Snow was falling, this was a proper hockey day! Tickets were still hard to get and that's if you can afford them. I purchased seats through Ticketmaster at a regular price, lower level, blue line at a cost of $250 each. It's top price these days.

The Canadiens have always been box office and that continues. The team was performing well and a win on the night would see them top the NHL. The pre-game presentation was impressive, the seats, though, were not. Very little leg room with not the best comfort, albeit the view was very good. The game was against the San Jose Sharks. We had seen this matchup before some years previously in California. To be really honest this game was one of the poorest I have witnessed, a very scrappy, stop-start affair, however, it did come to life in patches and a flowing move saw Plekanec finish at the far post to put the Canadiens ahead. Netminders Price (Mon) and Niemi (SJ) were in fine form. Defensively Montreal were a strong unit and I doubt there is a better player in the league who patrols the blue line than P.K. Subban. His sheer strength was more than evident giving Pavelski and Thornton little room up front for San Jose. I thought Thornton had a poor game and the Sharks overall did not look like play-off contenders. Late in the game Price secured his second shutout in three days with a terrific post to post pad save, and when the puck was cleared down the ice Gallagher sealed a 2-0 home win with an empty netter. Price picked up the first star award and rightly so. Karen had ticked off another NHL arena (just two to go).

You can actually walk underground through the city to the Bell Centre, however it can be confusing so having failed to negotiate the way back to our hotel post-game, we literally skated back; the pavements had become a sheet of ice.

It is always a thrill to be in Montreal for a game and we thoroughly enjoyed the experience again. One thing that did surprise me though about the Bell Centre was how much construction was going on around it. I think it is about to be engulfed by higher and wider buildings.

The following day we took a five-hour train ride to Toronto. Well, if you are in Canada you cannot pass up the chance to see the Leafs even if their season was going nowhere. The train though was painfully slow, struggling to get up a head of steam so we were pleased we did not take the one directly to New York City which takes ten hours. We were joined by friends Gerrie and Rhianna in Toronto. I had quite forgotten how cold it can get there and we decided on a walking tour which required more layers due to the minus 12 temperatures. Looking out over the Harbourfront area much of the river was still frozen, you can soon forget the cold though with all the bars and restaurants to choose from.

I have watched the Leafs in Toronto many times over the years but this time it seemed very different. The team was fourth from bottom of the NHL, their season had fallen away badly and the fans had given up. Replica shirts were on offer with 75% off and rumours were circulating that Phil Kessel would be traded at the end of the season. Prior to the start the Leafs organisation made a presentation to defenceman Eric Brewer. He also received a silver stick from the NHL to mark an achievement of being the 300th player to reach 1,000 NHL games; actually he had only joined the Leafs a few weeks previously.

The visitors were the Minnesota Wild who were in a different position with a chance to make the play-offs following their recent results. The first period seemed like an exhibition match, no hitting, little passion and the crowd... well, it really felt like a library. Predictably the Wild took the lead with a sloppy goal. In the past Leafs fans have been quick to voice their displeasure, but not this time, though one fan in front of me did suggest the team might try and cross their own blue line. At least the captain Dion Phaneuf stepped forward to fight Kyle Brodziak from the Wild. Unfortunately the spark it created for a short while was extinguished by a second Wild goal scored by Thomas Vanek who squeezed one through Bernier's pads. Actually the Leafs' netminder played well on the night. At least late in the third period the home fans had something to cheer when Gardiner stabbed the puck home following a rebound off Minnesota's keeper Dubnyk. That was as good as it got. The Leafs lost their seventh consecutive game and the end of the season could not come quick enough for all concerned in Toronto.

A sign of the times was when touts outside prior to the game were offering $200 tickets for $50. Why did I buy in advance? Anyway I finished the evening at Jack Astor's bar on front street where the staff are friendly and there is always a good atmosphere.

The following day we left for New York. Thankfully Toronto will have a new airport transit train in place shortly. This should have happened some years ago. Our Air Canada flight to LaGuardia followed by a taxi ride put us on 37th Street in Manhattan. This is just a ten-minute walk to Madison Square Garden.

The LA Kings were in town and desperate for points. The Stanley Cup holders had not found it easy to win games during the season. The Rangers who lost to the Kings in the cup final in 2014 were in opposite form, already on 99 points and joint top of the NHL. On the night though the Kings would do a number on the Rangers. An early New York goal by Mats Zuccarello put the visitors on the back foot, but the Kings showed their class with quick puck movement through the neutral zone and some clinical finishing. Cam Talbot (Rangers netminder) may have liked Regehr's equalising goal back but waves of pressure would result in more goals for Gaborik, Carter and Muzzin. There was a late Rangers reply by Hayes but this would not be enough. Madison Square Garden was full on the night as always with the crowd obviously enjoying their season. Injuries to Lundqvist and St Louis, however, had hindered matters more recently.

On to Long Island, New York. This time we stayed in the hotel next to the arena, Long Island railway to Westbury is 45 minutes and it's a $12 taxi from there. The team will move next season to play in Brooklyn at the Barclays Centre, so it is all winding down at the Nassau Coliseum and the fans are not that happy about it. I think the new arena will be easier to get to but I was informed it is not a place built for ice hockey and some seats will have a poor view.

The Islanders have enjoyed a good season on the ice although they had faltered of late. The Kings had come with us as part of a five-game road trip. I was surprised to see quite a lot of Los Angeles fans there. The game was much different to the one at Madison Square Garden, the Kings passing game was not allowed to flow and they went behind to a breakaway goal by Neilsen in the second period. The Kings missed out on a lengthy five on three but found an equaliser through Shore, his first of the season. The period was end to end hockey with the Kings taking the lead short-handed through Toffoli only for the Islanders defenceman Boychuk to blast one through from the point on a power play. The Kings would win it in the third period with a re-direction by Kopitar. The Islanders netminder Halak was unlucky to be on the losing side.

The Kings moved west to Minnesota still needing points to secure a play-off spot. For us it would be back to New York City and a train to Boston for the Saturday matinee show down with the New York Rangers.

We woke up to a view overlooking the Boston skyline. Snow was falling and to the locals this was just another day amongst others as the winter in the area had been one of the worst on record. It was a battle to walk to the TD Gardens. Many Rangers fans had made the trip but unfortunately their team failed to show up. Turnovers in their own zone, poor passing and a first period to forget left them 3-0 in arrears. Lundqvist had returned in goal but was beaten twice by Milan Lucic. Boston's netminder Rask was not able to complete the game through illness, however, his team-mates easily finished the job winning the game 4-2. To be honest it was never close and the Bruins missed three one on one chances. We had expected a much tighter game.

During the first period break we decided on a couple of hot dogs for lunch washed down with a beer. At the counter after queuing for some time, I was asked for ID required to order the beers. Having provided my photo driving licence I was refused the drinks as only a passport it seemed would suffice. The server was no more than an arrogant kid who seemed to delight in embarrassing us in front of others. I refused the hot dogs and took the matter up with a couple of staff members. One seemed to quote all kinds of local laws on sports/alcohol licencing, the other member of staff offered to bring beers to our seats. At this point, we had lost interest and returned to watch the game. We would never go to other countries and flout their laws and it is not in our nature to be anything but polite, I feel that common sense should have prevailed as we are aged 60 and 57! Such laws are surely in place to prevent over indulgence and underage drinking which may therefore lead to crowd disorder. Unfortunately, at the end of our trip, this did leave a sour taste. Boston is the only arena out of 116 that I have visited where I have been refused the opportunity to purchase a drink. It paints the organisation in quite a poor light in my opinion and I doubt we will return.

So that was the end of our trip, five NHL games in eight days. We had watched teams from the top end of the NHL, the play-off race was well and truly on, but in all honesty I thought the standard of ice hockey this time did not match the billing.

Karen will now have to wait for another trip to complete her quest to visit all the NHL arenas. She is now stuck on 29. Nashville awaits…

Season 2014/15 concluded with the Chicago Blackhawks winning the Stanley Cup. This is their third triumph in the last six years, a great achievement by the organisation.

FINAL WORD ON THE NHL

My overall view of the NHL is excellent and the standard of ice hockey is arguably the best in the world. The players have so much skill on the ice from speed and stick handling to physical presence, and total fitness plays a key role and they all seem to have the ability to read the game.

The arenas range from the old and historical to the new state of the art facilities. It's a good mix. My ideal is having the venues right downtown, walkable from your hotel with good pre-game bars available to allow you to mingle with the local fans.

I have, of course, made my thoughts known on the difficulty of obtaining tickets. Exchange programmes such as Ticketmaster and StubHub, I am now informed, have changed their systems which allows people outside of North America to purchase tickets. Cost is always a consideration of course. My personal choice is always to try and buy good seats and not have to sit high up. These type of tickets always seem to be over the $150 mark at least, and as a tout once told me if you want to watch the best sport you have to pay for it. At least that was his selling pitch. I find waiting until near the start of the game is the best way to get them to drop their asking price, but do not bet on it.

Whilst I was planning the March 2015 trip 'ticket prices' certainly jumped out at me. I managed to purchase some tickets direct from the clubs concerned, others via Ticketmaster and finally a couple via the Exchange Programme. Now I would admit that we did try to purchase half decent seats at games i.e. not in the 'nose bleeds' but, equally, we did not go for the best in the house. Even so it still cost us an average of $200 per ticket per game. The exchange rate did not help and add-on fees certainly bumped up the price. I mean $22 administration plus $7 'Will Call' collect fee? It gets a little silly. The NHL is now a premium event and perhaps trying to do a series of games in one trip is getting out of reach.

I have thoroughly enjoyed my experience over the years in visiting each NHL club. It is recommended for any ice hockey fan to make a trip if possible. I still intend to visit North America in the future to watch more games especially if a team relocates to a new arena.

CHAPTER 3

NOTTINGHAM PANTHERS AND BRITISH ICE HOCKEY

I have now been watching the Nottingham Panthers for almost 30 years. When I started looking back over this period, I realised that I would need to cover this part in three sections to allow me to fully evaluate it. The easiest way I felt would be to use the 'League Format' commencing with the Heineken sponsored league; this continued until 1993. The second section would be the Ice Hockey Super-League (ISL) 1996–2003, finishing with the Elite Ice Hockey League (EIHL) 2003–present. During this time, of course, we had the old arena on Lower Parliament Street before moving to the new National Ice Centre (NIC) built more or less on the same site in 2000.

It was during the 1986/87 season that I decided to attend a local game. It was now interesting me more than ever following my visit to Canada. The first problem was actually getting a ticket, "wait outside and someone will sell you one," I was told. Also the lady who sold 50/50 tickets was helpful in getting you a match ticket on the night. Lower Parliament Street was always sold out it seemed. The information proved to be correct and a friend and myself bought two tickets at the front in Block 3. To be perfectly honest I did not make any notes on the game and I do not even recall who the opposition was on the night, but what I do remember is being part of the experience. It seemed like we were on the ice. No netting or Plexiglass in place meant players sticks came very close as they battled on the boards, and at least three pucks flew out in our direction. I even threw one back. Nowadays of course you keep it. My friend just did not like to be this close up and spent part of the game in the bar. None of this was to put me off though and I was back the following weekend. In fact, I have been back ever since.

For years though at the old Ice Arena 'tickets' were always a problem, I got lucky in the mid-nineties when a friend allowed me to use his two reservation passes. This was not a season ticket of course so a need to buy match tickets a week in advance was still an issue. Queues meant you either had to miss some of the game or go into Nottingham to purchase during the week. It was quite simply not user friendly. Halfway up in Block 4 became my regular seat until the move to the new NIC in 2000. Prior to that I must have sat in just about every seat in the building so I got a good perspective on the game over the years. How did that compare to my first games at the NHL? Well to be perfectly honest in the early days I was not qualified to judge.

section 1 – Heineken League

By the time I had attended my first Panthers game late in 1986, the team had already won their first trophy since re-forming in 1980. The Panthers beat the Fife Flyers 5-4 in the early season 'Autumn Cup' sponsored by Norwich Union; the final was played at the NEC in Birmingham. Watching games in the old arena meant you would always be close to the action and I think this probably gave the impression the game was quicker than it actually was. Teams at that time were allowed three imports usually signed from North America. Fans' favourite Jimmy Keyes was already at the club, forward Fred Perlini and defenceman Terry Kurtenbach (TK) joined him. Other players on the team that I remember well were Randall Weber, Gavin Fraser, Nigel Rhodes and John Bremner. During the first few seasons I was quite amazed with how many goals were flying in. I watched games against the Murrayfield Racers (11-15), Slough Jets (16-6) and the Dundee Rockets (8-8). Actually I was informed that in the early eighties the Panthers actually won a game against Southampton scoring an incredible 31 goals.

Perlini finished top scorer in my first season with 108 goals (212 points). Netminding at that time was tough to put it mildly. Ian Woodward was in goal for the Panthers for 27 games and finished with a 6.3 (GAA) 'Goals Against Average'. Looking at this on the ice it became clear that teams were scoring too many cheap goals; 'shoot on site' seemed to be the policy and why not when shots were going in regularly from the blue line and even the red line on occasion. To me there didn't seem to be a coaching manual on defending, however, the fans loved it and it was great entertainment which had them on the edge of their seats. At the end of the 1986/87 season the Panthers finished third in a ten team league. Murrayfield Racers were champions with the Durham Wasps winning the play-offs.

The next two seasons would see contrasting fortunes for the Panthers. Imports were vital to all teams in the league, success or failure seemed to be built around these players, so when Jimmy Keyes retired and Fred Perlini joined the Fife Flyers it left a hole that coach Alex Dampier found difficult to fill. Terry Kurtenbach continued to lead the side but during the 1987/88 season Danny Bissonnette, Dave Ducharme, Pete Chiarelli and Mike Jeffrey all came in but failed to provide enough spark although Jeffrey's stats were not that bad. Players were released and Dampier signed Craig Melancon from the Streatham Redskins. He was a fiery player with good speed and scored 49 goals (123 points) from just 28 games. Even so this was a season best forgotten with the team finishing a poor sixth and losing 21 of their 36 league games including a record defeat in March 1988 when an injury hit side lost 23-1 at Whitley.

In addition they went on to lose all four play-off games. Brian Cox had been the main netminder and finished with a 7.4 GAA. The usual suspects would again claim the main trophies, the Murrayfield Racers and Durham Wasps. It was the Whitley Warriors that caught the eye though with quite a successful season, icing for them at that time was Canadian forward Mike

Babcock who netted 45 goals during that campaign. Babcock excelled later in his career with coaching, not just in the NHL with the Detroit Red Wings but also for Team Canada who won the gold medal at the Olympics in Vancouver in 2010, he is now the new coach of the Toronto Maple Leafs. I am sure he has never forgotten his time in Whitley Bay. The two other imports playing with Babcock were Scott Morrison and Luc Chabot.

Back with the Panthers and Coach Dampier needed to make changes if the club was to find a winning formula. Defence would need to be more of a priority and he went against the grain by signing a second import defenceman. The tall, imposing Darren Durdle came in to partner Terry Kurtenbach. Melancon did not return so a top class forward would be required and when first choice Bruce Thompson failed to impress, Paul Adey was signed from Briancon (France). Canadian Adey would of course go on to be a club legend. The 1988/89 season started to take shape. Dave Graham was now in goal and for a big man got down well and had a better GAA of 5.1 which helped Panthers finish third in the league behind the two main teams again. This time though the side would qualify for the play-off finals at the Wembley Arena. In their semi-final game on the Saturday they reached the final by beating the Whitley Warriors 8-6.

I decided to drive to Wembley on the Sunday to see the final against the Ayr Bruins. This was my first visit to this event and I have rarely missed one since. The arena was packed with fans from all over the country and not just from the top league. I loved the atmosphere! My memory fades somewhat when recalling the game but there were great celebrations by players and fans following the Panthers 6-3 win. Randall Weber, Gavin Fraser and Terry Kurtenbach were amongst the goals. The Bruins played their part until the third period when the Panthers pulled away. John McCrone had a good game in goal for Ayr, Frank Morris, Tommy Searle and John Kidd scored their goals. The Bruins player coach at that time was Rocky Saganuik, an ex NHL player and a real character, full of passion on and off the ice. He loved the game and it showed. He did an excellent job with the Bruins that season seeing off both Murrayfield and Durham to make the final. The Panthers though deserved their first play-off championship. It was nice to see great contributions during the season from Simon Perkins, Stuart Parker and Dwayne Keward before he retired. Paul Adey though announced his arrival with 88 goals (171 points) in just 40 games.

Looking back over that season I did retain some fabulous memories of when the Fife Flyers came to town. Some of their fans were dressed in kilts and they always seemed upbeat whatever the score was, and when it came to having a pre-game beverage, well, they had no equal in how much they could consume. The team was always good to watch and it was during that season they went with three imports from Czechoslovakia (this was before the country was split), Vincent Lukac, Milan Figala and Jindrich Kokrment. These were skilled players and even then I noticed how different their style was compared to the usual North American imports.

These first few years had given me an insight into the game of 'Ice Hockey'. I did struggle for some time though over systems, matchups and line changes, but penalties would leave me shaking my head the most. Tripping, interference and cross checking, well it all seemed straightforward until you factor in roughing, fighting, instigation, delay of game and then accidental high sticking, but if you draw blood, well, that carries an extra two minutes. Too many men, well it goes on, equipment, abuse of an official, I guess the crowd would fill the box on that one. In the nineties we had another 'too many imports on the ice'. The home fans would call this, only on one side though. If all this was confusing let's try other stoppages during the game like icing (sometimes waved off) then two line passes thankfully now gone. I was never informed that a degree of some kind was needed to understand the game, and even now fans around me cry out "where's the goalie gone?" when the referee has his arm raised to indicate a penalty against the opposing team. Actually some older fans like myself will also re-call some penalties that were issued following a 'stick measurement'. If a coach thought an opposing player had an illegal stick he could ask the referee to measure the curve and width I believe. There are actual rules on what the maximum should be, however, the coach needed to hope he was correct because if not the penalty would go against his team. Mike Blaisdell used this tactic more than once.

The next few years would not register in the memory in terms of success for the Nottingham Panthers. The 1989/90 season started with the surprise departure of Darren Durdle, and his replacements, Yves Beaudin and Keith Stewart, did not have the same impact. Panthers finished sixth in the league, however, they did reach the semi-final of the play-offs at Wembley only to lose a close encounter 5-4 against Tony Hand and his Murrayfield Racers. A real highlight for me during this season was the continued emergence of youngster Simon Hunt, best described as a pocket battleship. His orders it seemed were to hit anything that moved. Opposing players were in for a rough ride and boy did he get the crowd going as during the season he racked up 100 minutes in penalties. This aside though Hunt could play and belied his small stature by having a wicked slap shot hitting 19 goals in his first full season. Paul Adey would dominate the main scoring though with an incredible 96 goals (184 points). It was during this season that the Durham/Murrayfield dominance would be broken. Enter the Cardiff Devils. The Welsh side had gained promotion and then strengthened their side tempting both Ian and Stephen Cooper away from Durham. Player coach at the time was John Lawless and when he added Steve Moria to the line-up they became a force. The Devils won the league title losing just three games and then completed the double by knocking over the Racers in the Wembley final.

The standard of the league was now starting to improve. The BIHA agreed a fourth import per team from the start of the 1990/91 season, however, eligibility would have to be defined through residency/parentage i.e. qualified to play for Great Britain. These rules would change again over the coming seasons which to be honest caused some confusion. The Panthers did not get involved during the 1990/91 season instead staying with the three imports. Terry Kurtenbach and Paul Adey would be joined initially by Rick Strachan but after 31 games he was replaced by Todd Bidner, coach Dampier citing 'lack of goals' within the team. The loss of Nigel Rhodes was also a factor in this. It was Paul Adey who carried the goal threat scoring 101 goals with TK weighing in with 41 goals, but despite these two excellent players Panthers would again finish sixth and also fail to reach the Wembley finals weekend.

The Durham Wasps reaction to the Cardiff Devils arriving on the scene and claiming trophies the previous season was to simply win the treble. With the Autumn Cup and League Championship secured, they beat surprise finalists Peterborough Pirates in the Wembley play-off final. Rick Brebant led the way with a 209-point season. The Cooper brothers had returned from Cardiff and Mike Blaisdell had also joined. He was a hard-nosed player with 343 NHL games in his locker. For the Pirates it had been a great achievement to reach a Wembley final under the leadership of Rocky Saganiuk. He had already done a great job with the Ayr Bruins but this was a terrific achievement. One of their best players at the time I recall was Danny Shea.

The Wembley finals weekend started to take on a new meaning for me from the early nineties, with the league being sponsored by Heineken and my company having a large contract with Whitbread. Cue an invite to the weekend as a guest. Hospitality was run by TGI Fridays so food, drink etc., seats at the games were top class – a lucky break! Mostly though I enjoyed the weekends because of the fans, and if I had to pick a bunch that live long in the memory then the 'Sollihull Barons' would top the league.

T-shirts printed for the occasion 'No Bar's Too Far' was one of the cleaner versions. I remember Swansea City Fans (their team was playing a minor cup final at Wembley Stadium) trying to moon at the Barons fans from their coach. No contest. Not a great sight but the West Midlanders won hands down or bottoms up if you prefer. Actually I have no recollection of Solihull ever getting to the Wembley finals weekend but the fans still came to see ice hockey as did fans of other clubs. The finals were staged at the arena for 13 years in total until 1996. I thought it was a great occasion.

The Heineken sponsored years were winding down; season 1991/92 proved to be a better year for the Panthers. Dan Dorian joined the club and from just 48 games posted 200 points. Dorian was a real live wire with an eye for goal. Chris Kelland joined the defence as a reclassified import/Dual National (I have probably described that completely wrong). Other players were also making their mark in the team. Graham Waghorn played 63 games on defence and a young Ashley Tait came onto the scene. Hunt racked up 261 penalty minutes, and now with Kelland (211 penalty minutes) Dampier had added some toughness. The Panthers were having quite a successful season, firstly winning the Autumn Cup beating the Humberside Seahawks 7-5 in the final. A second place finish in the league to champions Durham was followed by a winning play-off campaign and then reaching the final at Wembley by knocking out the Peterborough Pirates in the semi-final 7-3. The final was a pulsating affair with Durham retaining their crown with a 7-6 win.

So just when the club looked to be making inroads at the top end of the competitions, things started to go wrong. At the start of the 1992/93 season the ice plant broke down at the arena and home games until the middle of October had to be played elsewhere. I recall travelling to the Autumn Cup quarter-final away at the Basingstoke Beavers on the Saturday and then to the return leg at home. Well actually at Hull the following day. Panthers did win through to the semi-finals but went out over two legs to the Devils. The Nottingham Panthers were then thrown into disarray when Dan Dorian left the club having already scored 50 goals by December; coach Alex Dampier then resigned after seven years with the organisation. The fans were left shaking their heads. The new coach was Kevin Murphy who was known as a disciplinarian and Selmar Odelein joined as the new import. All of this though paled into insignificance when young player Gary Rippingale sadly died at the end of October and the club retired his number three shirt.

Despite all of this the Panthers still managed to finish third in the league and reached the semi-final stage at Wembley when Dan Dorian came back to haunt the club; playing for his new team, the Humberside Seahawks, he scored two goals plus one assist as the Hawks reached the final. Coach Murphy was sacked a few days afterwards. The Cardiff Devils returned to complete the treble. I guess the fans did have one good memory from a poor season: a moment during a home game against the Whitley

Warriors erupted when Selmar Odelein came face to face with Mike Rowe. Now Rowe had for some time been knocking players around in the league including Odelein's brother who played for the Bracknell Bees. A huge mistake and the Nottingham crowd demanded blood. Actually it seemed like one punch and Rowe was left prostrate on the ice. It was one of those nights when you could never remember the match, just that moment.

I think at this time I had not been enjoying the games as much and at the start of the 1993/94 season I really questioned just what was going on at the club. When the captain Terry Kurtenbach was not retained, it left the fans in disbelief. He joined the Romford Raiders and returned to the arena when the Raiders played in the Autumn Cup. In those days the players' names were announced prior to the start of the game and each player would then move to the blue line. When Terry Kurtenbach's name was called out the cheers and applause went on and on. It was an amazing tribute and well deserved and it carried on at the end of the game when he collected his 'Man of the Match' award.

Mike Blaisdell took up the reins as the Panthers coach at the start of the 1993/94 season. Ross Lambert, who was a combative player joined alongside a new defenceman, Garth Premak. He was probably the nearest to replacing Terry Kurtenbach with his style of play. It was to be an injury hit season though particularly when the main man, Paul Adey, was 'submarined' in an away game in Whitley. Terry Ord was allegedly the villain of the peace and Adey suffered cruciate ligament damage. I remember the return match against the Warriors when the fans were baying for revenge, however, Ord was left out of the line-up. Nigel Rhodes had returned to the club and put up good numbers with excellent support from Ashley Tait and Randall Weber, but the loss of Adey meant Panthers would finish outside the top three in the league and they went on to suffer a bad defeat (8-0) to the Sheffield Steelers in the play-off semi-final at Wembley. Adey did ice during that game, which was a great credit to him, but he was not fit and consequently would miss the Pool A World Championships in Bolzano where he would have played for Great Britain. The Steelers lost in the final to the double winners, Cardiff Devils.

Coach Blaisdell strengthened his side at the start of the 1994/95 season as Rick Brebant joined Adey in attack which would see them post a combined 205 goals. The hard working Ross Lambert joined in with 53 goals and with contributions from Tait, Weber, Hunt and Belanger it was no surprise that the Panthers topped the league scoring charts with 372 goals. It was though the Sheffield Steelers who would win the league and play-off titles. I remember visiting the 'House of Steel' in those days with massive crowds and a Steelers team full of talent. Ken Priestlay (ex NHL) had joined the likes of Steve Nemeth and Tim Cranston and in defence were players like Andre Malo, Ron Shudra and, of course, Chris Kelland. When Tony Hand joined they basically became unstoppable going on to win the title three years in a row. The Panthers would taste success by winning the Autumn Cup in December 1994 knocking over the Cardiff Devils 7-2 in the final. A third place finish in the league was followed by qualification to the Wembley play-offs, however, they went down 11-7 to Murrayfield in the semi-final despite Paul Adey netting five times in that game.

So on to the final season (1995/96) of the first phase before the ISL was formed. Darren Durdle returned to the club but both Lambert and Brebant would depart. Lack of finance plus injuries to key players would provide a tough challenge for Blaisdell and fourth place in the league was quite reasonable. What hurt the most though was reaching two finals and losing both to the Sheffield Steelers the Autumn Cup (2-5) and a Wembley play-off final (4-5). Blaisdell was himself pressed into action and scored 35 goals, Adey, yet again, would top the statistics with 154 points. Scott O'Connor was now in goal and had an excellent season.

It had now been almost ten years since I had started watching ice hockey so I was starting to build up some knowledge and understanding of the game. The standard and quality of British ice hockey was improving and was about to get even better with the ISL. Eight teams would compete in the league, the Manchester Storm would play at the excellent MEN Arena with 17,000 plus capacity, Sheffield, Newcastle (Cobras), Basingstoke, Bracknell, Cardiff and Ayr would all join the Nottingham Panthers. I looked forward with great anticipation.

Firstly though, a look back at my highlights of the first period. What jumped out at me over this time was how dedicated ice hockey fans are. The support of their team and love of the sport has no bounds it seems. Travel, team shirts etc., 50/50 tickets, you name it, and fans buy it, shirt auctions being quite unbelievable. As I travelled to different rinks, this became apparent and in addition to their dedication they create a great atmosphere at games. All this certainly stood out to me. Of course visiting different rinks was an eye opener. Durham with little and no protection from the puck and a real partisan crowd, Whitley Bay late on a Sunday night was like stepping back in time and Murrayfield with needing several layers on but loving the 'Stovies', most rinks were originally built for public skating.

Prior to the arena clubs coming in, at Nottingham your Panthers ticket also included skating after the game. I did have a go (in a fashion) and it made the night for a lot of the fans. I was told that before my time if you did not skate you picked up a 50 pence refund on the way out. I guess when Panthers fans started to visit the 'House of Steel', it came as a bit of a shock when you compared it to all the old buildings. Some have never taken to it, I actually like a night there, Mr. Simms included.

Player wise I started to understand the role of individuals on the ice. Imports were under pressure to perform to a high standard but in the early days discovering British talent would enhance the team's success rate. The Cooper brothers, David Longstaff and Nicky Chinn are names that roll off the tongue. There were more but none would compare with Tony Hand, and much has been written regarding his possible chance to play in the NHL. My view is that he is simply the finest player I have watched in British ice hockey. He reads the game like no other; he plays with a style that dominates the ice, head up, always looking for that killer pass and he could thread such a pass through the eye of a needle. For me he was always in a different class.

I guess my final thoughts on the early years would be incidents that stick in the memory from the old ice arena in Nottingham. If trying to buy tickets for future games was an issue then purchasing a drink between periods was quite simply problematic. By the time you got served and tried to re-take your seat, stewards would cite the licensing laws of not being allowed to take a drink to your seat after the period had started. I was even asked to knock back a glass of wine before being allowed to take my seat. Now I accept the laws etc. but if you cannot be served quickly enough... well, it all became quite farcical.

On the ice I do recall some real altercations but none stick out as much as after a game between the Panthers and Devils in the nineties. During the handshake at the conclusion of the game Shannon Hope headbutted Chris Kelland and all hell broke loose. There was blood everywhere. This must have been due to something that had occurred during previous meetings and the incident came as a bit of a shock to the fans as no one saw it coming. Kelland most definitely did not see it coming. Despite this Kelland still played at Hull the following night and got into a fight with one of the Johnson brothers. Hockey players never walk away it appears.

Section 2 – Ice Hockey Super League (ISL)

The league was officially launched in London; there was even a photo-shoot in Trafalgar Square with a player from each organisation wearing a team shirt.

Sir John Hall was involved having originally purchased the Durham Wasps before moving the club to the arena in Newcastle. They would then become the Cobras.

Sky Sports also got involved (1996–1999) showing some live games presented at that time by the excellent Jane Hoffen. It was all done quite professionally. The league did manage to find a major sponsor in 1998, Sekonda, which would continue until 2002.

So on to the first season 1996/97. This league would represent a huge step up in playing standards. A cap on import players was no more it seemed. All eight teams in the league set about recruitment in a much different way and getting this right would be vital in terms of gaining success during the season, though questions were already being asked about how financially viable this would be.

For the Nottingham Panthers, Durdle departed for Germany, Adey and Premak remained along with British players Tait, Hunt, Weber and Waghorn. New players joined the club including Marty Dallman, Greg Hadden, Jeff Hoad, Derek Laxdal, Mike Bishop and netminder Trevor Robins. If you included coach Mike Blaisdell, Panthers would use 14 imports during the season and they would not be alone either with other clubs having similar levels.

It was a fairly slow start to the season with players

settling in around the league. Early success was to come for the Panthers in the Benson and Hedges Cup, following qualification from the group stages. They beat the Cardiff Devils (quarter-final) and Sheffield Steelers (semi-final) over two legs.

The final would be at the 'House of Steel' against the Ayr Scottish Eagles. The fans were on their feet in just 29 seconds when Laxdal opened the scoring. Bishop, Morgan, Hadden and Premak would all find the net in a 5-3 win to secure the trophy. The Eagles were a good side coached by Jim Lynch with some notable players in their squad like Scott Young, Jiri Lala, Ryan Kummu, Angelo Catenano, Matt Hoffman and Alan Schuler. It was already becoming clear that the quality of ice hockey had moved up several gears. The game had become much quicker and the Panthers definitely had one of the fastest skaters in the league in Brent Bobyck. It was goaltending that stood out to me and with Trevor Robins you suddenly had a 'brick in the wall'. He was a totally focused individual and opponents needed to watch out if they tried to get in his face. He played 45 games in the season with a 2.8 GAA.

Continuing on with the league part of the season and the Panthers would finish in fourth place with 45 points from 42 games. Cardiff were the first winners of the ISL with Sheffield second and Ayr third. It was these three teams that the Panthers would find hard to beat during the season. However, in a four-team play-off group the Panthers managed to get through to the last four.

The format for the finals was now completely different; firstly it was held at the MEN Arena but over two weekends. Panthers would again face the Ayr Scottish

Eagles, this time in the semi-final, and what an epic-battle it was. Ayr had been in the lead 4-1 and 5-2 but Mike Bishop with two goals and Neil Morgan with one levelled the game. These goals came inside three minutes late in the third period. At 5-5 the teams played out five periods of overtime without a winner (no penalty shots in those days). It must have been midnight when finally in the sixth overtime period Jeff Hoad scored a short-handed goal for the Panthers to secure a place in the final. Robins faced 74 shots would you believe? I recall my friend from Warrington had missed his last train so I had to drive the long way back arriving home at 4am.

The following week it was back to the same venue for the final against the Steelers. A great pre-game atmosphere was created by the fans at the pub under the arches in Manchester near the MEN Arena (no longer there I believe). At the final no overtime was required as Alex Dampier coached the Steelers to a 3-1 play-off trophy success, Frank Kovacs with one of their goals. The Steelers were a good side, strong in defence with Mike O'Connor, Ron Shudra and Rob Wilson, physical presence in Corey Beaulieu, experience in Ken Priestlay, Jamie Leach and Tim Cranston and, orchestrated by Tony Hand, they were tough to beat.

The first ISL season had still been a success for the Panthers. Paul Adey was the leading scorer with 38 goals.

There were a few notable events that took place during the season. Plexiglass was installed at the old Panthers arena and during a TV game Paul Adey scored to reach 1,000 points. Cue an on-ice presentation for a terrific achievement. Finally the Manchester Storm created a British attendance record. It was a game in February 1997 against the Steelers and 17,245 were inside and it was reported 1,500 were locked out.

The 1997/98 season was memorable for all the wrong reasons. It had been announced that the Nottingham Panthers were in debt and the club was put up for sale. I recall some bucket collections were made by fans in an attempt to help. Eventually, the Nottingham Panthers were sold to 'Aladdin Management'. Head of this consortium was Neil Black.

The Super League also suffered some problems. A continental tie up failed to materialise so an additional cup 'Express' sponsored by the *Daily Express* came in. I thought it all seemed a bit disjointed. Panthers did not get anywhere near any of the titles. The side did suffer some injuries to be fair. The Ayr Scottish Eagles nailed all four trophies in a dominant year.

During the season we had one of the more amusing moments in the crowd. Block 4 regulars were never short of a word or two about everything ice hockey. At one particular game Derek Laxdal, (Panthers forward) invited a few comments with his less than effective display on the ice. Unfortunately, a rather feisty lady took exception to these witty words and made it quite clear she was not in agreement. Well I guess she would see it differently as she turned out to be Mrs. Laxdal. Well Mr. Laxdal must have been clearly upset by the comments made as he left at the end of that season to join the Sheffield Steelers.

The 1998/99 season was really quite a successful campaign for the Panthers especially given that their financial situation was still far from secure, this despite having new owners. Garth Premak retired and several new players came in including Mark Kolesar who had played more than 30 games for the Toronto Maple Leafs in the NHL. Graham Garden also joined from Basingstoke. I always thought he was one of the hardest working players ever to play for the club. Amongst the new signings was Jarret Zukiwsky and he racked up 169 minutes in penalties, I would suggest mostly for fighting. He never stepped away from a situation. He seemed to have quite a unique style of getting into his opponent with a short burst of combination punches. It did not always work in his favour but he was certainly entertaining.

Talking of fights, I recall Paul Adey getting involved in a real tasty affair with Ivan Matulik. Both players were so incensed with each other that they started again immediately on leaving the penalty box. I don't think you could have picked a winner.

During the season Panthers added some strength to their line-up with Jason Weaver and Darcy Loewen; in defence Corey Beaulieu and Eric Dubois also joined the ranks. Blaisdell had recruited well and it paid off with some success winning the Autumn Cup and finishing runners up in the Express Cup. Following a third place finish in the league the Panthers reached the final of the play-offs at the MEN Arena. They lost out 2-1 to the Devils with that man again Ivan Matulik scoring both the Devils' goals.

One certain memory sticks out at me from the season, a game against Newcastle Riverkings at home.

Panthers defender Corey Beaulieu had an altercation with Rob Trumbley. Now Beaulieu was a tough player but Trumbley hit him with an 'uppercut' and his legs just buckled. Trumbley was quite a character and not adverse to a bout or two. I even recall where the incident occurred, just to the right of Block 4 in front of our seats. Strange how you retain certain memories of game incidents (no idea what the score was by the way).

The Manchester Storm won the ISL title; they had excellent coaching with Kurt Kleinendorst and Daryl Lipsey. The team was strong throughout the campaign winning 30 games. In goal was Frank Pietrangelo who was one of the best at that time, and other star names I recall were Mike Morin, Brad Rubachuk, Jeff Tomlinson and Jonathan Weaver.

The 1999/2000 season would be the last at the old Parliament Street stadium and it started off in the worse possible way. Neil Black cut the wage bill drastically and players left in droves including Trevor Robins who certainly left a big hole to fill. For me though the biggest loss would be Paul Adey. The club's all-time record scorer quite simply could not be replaced. Mike Blaisdell struggled to put a decent side out to compete and by November he had gone. He joined the Sheffield Steelers as their new coach.

Alex Dampier returned as Panthers coach, however, the fans were far from happy with Black who seemed to be biding his time until the move to the new arena. Jordan Willis had taken over in goal and a couple of decent players came in like Stephen Cooper and David Struch but overall the Panthers were a shadow of recent times finishing sixth in the league and losing all six play-off games.

The season would of course always be remembered for the last game at the old arena. It was a game they would lose 2-1 to Newcastle. Fans turned up with screwdrivers, hammers and saws, you name it. At the end of the game anything and everything in the arena seemed to be taken apart and taken home by the fans. I remember driving along Canal Street after the game and seeing people with benches, signs and all sorts; everyone had great memories (and now mementos) of the old place.

One of the main highlights of the season for me was the Bracknell Bees as they won the ISL title. This was an incredible achievement for such a small club. Led by coach Dave Whistle they had some excellent players like Paxton Schulte, Todd Kelman, Shane Johnson and Matt Cote. Unfortunately after their triumph the Bees lost their coach and some of their players to the newly formed Belfast Giants.

Another new team the London Knights burst onto the scene and their head coach was Chris McSorley. Now he was certainly a character. I recalled him being in charge of the Las Vegas Thunder in the IHL. He put together a tough side with players like Darren Banks, Andy Bezeau, Mike Ware, Barry Nieckar and Paul Rushforth. In addition, they were full of talent with Neal Martin, Rob Kenny and ex-Panthers Robins, Hoad and Kolesar. The Knights won the play-off championship, however, it was their semi-final game against Ayr that stole the headlines. It was a really tough game and this was exemplified when Andy Bezeau 'lost it'. He got so wound up he just went for the Ayr bench on his own, trading punches with at least five Eagles including Rob Trumbley who had joined them. Bezeau was not the biggest of players but still managed to total over 3,000 penalty minutes in his career. I think we lack these kind of characters nowadays in ice hockey.

For the Panthers, credit must be given to the team during the season for reaching the Challenge Cup final. This was played as a one-off final at the London Docklands Arena, however, it was Blaisdell and the Steelers who would triumph 2-1. Actually the tickertape came down from the roof with two seconds left on the clock. It would not have made any difference of course, just one of those things that stick in the mind.

The Nottingham Panthers would now move on to a new era. The brand new arena (NIC) was ready and open days were held to allow you to view the facilities and apply for season tickets if you wished. I decided not to purchase one preferring to buy each week and sit in different areas. The arena held 7000 and we probably had 3000 fans, but this would of course increase with no restrictions. I took the view though to see how it went. I think the previous season had left me less than enthusiastic.

Season 2000/01 was the first time the Nottingham Panthers would play at their new home – the National Ice Centre (NIC). The facility had cost around £43 million and funding was provided by the City Council and National Lottery. Sadly changes to the area would mean the end for the Cricket Players pub. I remember spending far too much time and money in there over the

NOTTINGHAM PANTHERS AND BRITISH ICE HOCKEY

years. Nowadays The Castle and Bunker's Hill are the main attractions.

It was quite an eventful season and not for the right reasons. The ISL now consisted of nine teams with the addition of the newly formed Belfast Giants. A lower wage cap of £450,000 for the season was introduced and three points were now available for a win. The Panthers added new players to the roster: Barry Nieckar, P.C. Drouin and Jimmy Paek all joined with Kevin Hoffman and Robert Nordmark coming in later.

In truth it was a quite dreadful campaign for the team. Dampier even brought in an assistant coach in Peter Woods but to no avail. The Club finished eighth in the league and just qualified for the play-offs. However, that was in dramatic fashion when Nordmark fired home to secure a 2-2 draw at Newcastle with just four seconds left. No headway was made in the play-offs losing five of their six games. This in addition to 30 league defeats summed it all up. On the plus side attendances had now gone up to an average of 4,259.

Fans will of course always remember a certain battle (literally) against the Steelers in February 2001. Following a hit on Greg Hadden there was a bench clearance and a mass brawl. It went on and on. I remember Barry Nieckar stripping down to the waist like a prizefighter. He must have taken on half of Sheffield. But it was his personal fight with Scott Allison that stood out. Referee Moray Hanson eventually ordered both teams to their dressing rooms without finishing the period. After a delay of almost one hour the game restarted. Nine players in total were ejected, this included the Steelers netminder Eoin McInerney. In addition both coaches (Woods & Blaisdell) were also thrown out. Penalty minutes in the game reached 453 (404 in one period). Panthers who were behind in the game did win 6-4, it was the Steelers though that went on to win all four competitions. Controversy would follow them when they were found guilty of exceeding the wage cap and consequently stripped of their trophies.

This was not the first time there had been bad blood between the two sides. I recall an incident a couple of years before when a game in Sheffield erupted. Blake Knox (not the biggest player) punched the Steelers hard case Mike Ware. Cue an incredible hulk moment. Ware went nuts. He chased Knox all over the ice before being restrained. Ware was not to be messed with. He once had a spell with the Hannover Scorpions in the DEL. During a pre-game warm-up he took revenge on an opposing player. Allegedly he was arrested at the rink and deported. Later he played for the Knights and Devils.

During the season I attended a matinee game on New Year's Eve. It was at the House of Steel where the Steelers hosted the Manchester Storm. Now to this day it remains probably the best British league game I have seen. It just seemed to have everything, totally incident packed, and over 7000 were in attendance including hundreds of Manchester fans.

At one point it was announced that there was a bad snowstorm raging outside. But I doubt anyone left. Goals were flying in at both ends as the teams were committed to attack. It was a real physical encounter and eventually it really kicked off. Players were throwing punches at each other but there was no bench clearance. However, with Rob Trumbley in the penalty box two Steelers seemed to set about the Storm's Corey Spring. The next part was like a scene from a film. Suddenly the penalty box door opened, Trumbley came flying out and literally dived on the back of Steelers Paul Beraldo, and he flattened him! All hell then broke loose with fighting all over the ice. Dennis Vial and Scott Metcalf (Steelers) at this point totally lost it. Trumbley was public enemy number one, not that it seemed to bother him as he was still trading punches with Beraldo on his way to being ejected. I don't think Beraldo knew where he was. Referee Kirkham handled it well. The game still went both ways until a late Steelers marker secured a narrow 7-6 win. I really enjoyed the game, real passion and total commitment.

So far I have only touched on referees in the British leagues. Much criticism has been levelled at the stripeys from across the fan bases. Well, I really do not share these views. Often it is too easy to blame others when your own team fails to perform. Do we, as fans of the game, really know all the rules inside out? I would doubt it. Of course officials make mistakes, as we all do. In the past we have been fortunate to have had some excellent officials. From the early days of Nico Toeman who set a high standard, Moray Hanson, Simon Kirkham and the late Mick Curry have all stood out to me. I have been at games in the European leagues where the officials were pelted with objects from the stands. In the NHL (even with the two-man system) I have witnessed outrage amongst fans at various venues. Our officials would probably benefit from attending clinics in North America but who is going to fund this level of training?

The next two seasons (2001/02 and 2002/03) would unfortunately be the last for the ISL. Problems had already surfaced when Newcastle and Cardiff went into liquidation, so season 2001/02 would be a seven-team league. For the Panthers Paul Adey was now in charge. It was a change of personnel again for the team – Darren Maloney, Patrik Wallenberg and Lee Jinman came in. It was though a fairly average season for the club finishing fourth, and they failed to figure on the trophy list. During the season foreign opposition provided good entertainment for me. There were two friendlies against top Russian sides, AZ Kazan Bars and Dynamo Moscow, the Panthers holding the legendry Moscow side to a 3-3 draw.

Also during the season the ISL organised a new competition the 'Ahearne Trophy'. Each ISL team would play two games against the German Ice Hockey League (DEL). Panthers lost a tight game 2-1 to Iserlohn Roosters but triumphed 3-2 against Dusseldorf. I thought these were excellent games. I also went to games at Sheffield (v Oberhausen) and Manchester twice to see Iserlohn (again) and Eisbaren Berlin. Both these games ended in a draw. The Rooster fans were very funny in Manchester. They all brought towels with them and placed them on rows of empty seats, therefore mimicking British holidaymakers by the pool. It was all in good humour. The DEL won the trophy 16-12 on points. It was a really good effort by the British sides when you consider the strength of the German top league.

The start of the 2002/03 season was fraught with problems for the ISL. Manchester and Ayr hit financial and rink problems and would therefore not be able to continue. This left a five-team league. In addition Bracknell announced they would drop down to a lower league the following season. It had become obvious the ISL would cease at the end of the campaign. The Steelers won the final ISL title just edging out the Giants by one point. The Giants though went on to win the play-off trophy beating the London Knights 5-3. Panthers lost in the semi-final and finished third in the league.

For me the season was dominated by penalties. To be honest I expected nothing less when the Panthers acquired Dody Wood (249 minutes) and Jason Clarke (238 minutes). To add to Barry Nieckar (222 minutes), even Scott Allison (150 minutes) joined. At least players like Jinman, Hadden and Cadotte were allowed to play and put up good numbers. Actually this Panthers side were very strong that season with players like Briane Thompson (even he had 153 penalty minutes), Kristian Taubert, Eric Charron and Marc Hussey.

Inevitably suspensions would hit the club. As mentioned in my Continental Cup section, fans in Belfast were irate when a game in October 2002 erupted at the end, cue a mass brawl. Paxton Schulte was injured and the Northern Irish fans have never forgotten.

During the final ISL season there was another European series of games for the Ahearne Trophy. This time it was against the Norway Elite League. This time the British sides easily won the cup winning eight of the ten games played. I remember watching Panthers beat

Sparta Sarpsborg 11-3. The Norwegians seemed scared to death of the Panthers, now I wonder why…

An interesting footnote – attendances were up 9% for the season at an average of 4,426.

For many of my early years of watching ice hockey I used to really enjoy reading the *Ice Hockey News Review*. It was an excellent publication that became weekly. It covered all the leaguers with individual statistics. The editor was the late Vic Batchelder who was a journalist and loved the game. He was inducted into Ice Hockey's Hall of Fame. I recall another journalist, the late Norman De-Mesquita who covered ice hockey at that time and another excellent writer who was also inducted into the Hall of Fame. Unfortunately I do not believe there are any UK magazines available these days which are attributed to the game. Online blogs/forums seem to be an easy and less costly way to communicate. Personally I wish we could have both.

section 3 – elite ice Hockey League (EIHL)

Dramatic changes were needed to ensure the future of British ice hockey. The highest standard possible should be aimed for. However it needed to be sustainable in the longer term. In particular clubs needed to be financially stable. In addition more emphasis should be placed on developing young British talent. All this sounded quite easy on paper. However, the newly named Elite Ice Hockey League had to be put together in a rather hasty fashion. The London Knights did not continue so only three teams remained from the ISL. Five new teams joined – Coventry Blaze, Basingstoke Bison, newly formed London Racers (who would play at Lee Valley Ice Centre), Manchester Phoenix (who only managed one season initially at this level) and finally the Cardiff Devils would return.

There still seemed to be some issues around affecting the League's acceptance by the IIHF. There was even some talk of another team instead of the Panthers operating from the NIC (like that was ever going to happen!). Anyway it seemed to get sorted out and much credit should be given to those in charge for working tirelessly to make it work.

The Panthers would be much changed. There were more British players in the side (I could only remember Paul Moran from the previous season). David Clarke signed along with Marc Levers. In goal Mika Pietila was replaced by Niklas Sundberg. One interesting addition was John Craighead, a tall, imposing player with an Afro hairstyle to match. Some fans even wore wigs to the game to support him. I had actually seen Craighead before in Nuremberg. Greg Hadden had decided to retire. He was the ISL leading scorer. He spent seven years with the Panthers who gave him a testimonial. He was a really popular player with the fans. It was decided by the club to retire his No 11 shirt, well deserved!

New league, new season but the same winners, the Sheffield Steelers, easily won the league title and completed the double by beating the Panthers 2-1 in the play-off final. Even so it was a good season for the Nottingham club finishing runners up in the league and play-offs. They won the Challenge Cup at Sheffield with Kim Ahlroos scoring an overtime winner to beat the Steelers 4-3 on aggregate.

I had some concerns about the standard of ice hockey and how it would hold up against the last seven years of watching the ISL. Well it may have been too early to judge but I thought it was a reasonable start. There was however a drop in the average attendance to 3,915.

The following three to four seasons became a little different for me in terms of watching the game. The company I worked for acquired a hospitality box at the NIC. I agreed a deal to entertain clients etc. at all ice hockey games until the company was sold in 2006. I looked after people at over 100 games. Actually it proved to be less glamorous than it sounded, contacting and meeting individuals who were often late, organising tickets/passes, ordering food/drink, explaining the game to some who were only there for the beer. Well, to be honest, it was a quite a commitment which I was delighted to relinquish at the end. I mean how many times can you explain the offside rule and be met with a blank expression. Actually it was Karen that highlighted the point to me when we attended a game in 2007 and sat in Block 4. It was the first time in a few years that I had enjoyed a game with no stress. It seemed I had become so embroiled in making sure everyone was enjoying the evening that I lost sight of what was important to me.

The 2004/05 season proved to be quite different in many ways. Nottingham Panthers competed in the Continental Cup in Amiens (I cover this in that section). A British player actually topped the Club's goal charts when David Clarke recorded 61 points including 31 goals. Clarke has a very effective slap shot with some real power attached. Later in the season, due to a lock-out in the NHL, two players joined the Panthers playing over 20 games each. Nick Boynton (Boston) was a defenceman. I thought he looked a little unfit at first but it was clear he was a talented player. He scored an excellent goal against the Coventry Blaze in the play-off final at the NIC. Unfortunately for the Panthers former player Ashley Tait netted the overtime winner to complete his side's treble winning season. Ian Moran (Boston) also wore the Panthers shirt. He had excellent skating ability as all NHL players do. I really do not think he had enough time to make an impact to be fair. He scored two goals during his 21-game stay.

During the season there was another experiment of note with 'cross league games' with the British National League (BNL). It was nice to see different opposition. In fact two of those sides, Newcastle Vipers and Edinburgh Races, joined the Elite League for the 2005/06 campaign. Unfortunately the London Races folded soon after the start, but at least it was back to an eight-team league.

Sadly for the Panthers, coach Paul Adey would not be part of it. Neil Black did not retain his services instead turning back to Mike Blaisdell. I found it all quite strange and it came as no surprise that it turned out to be short-lived. In fairness Panthers did manage a third place finish in the league which was acceptable given the injury list during the season. Dan Tessier had signed and put up good numbers. However, the lure of the Swiss franc in Lausanne meant he would only play 23 games. The team did not make the play-off weekend, which was hard on the fans, as it now seemed to be an annual event at the NIC. At least there was a surprise winner in the Newcastle Vipers who had already finished league runners up to Belfast. The Vipers had some top players that season. In goal was Trevor Koenig, British players Jonathan Weaver, David Longstaff and Michael Tasker, with imports Paul Ferone and Andre Payette. They were quite a strong outfit!

Season 2006/07 and suddenly the Elite League would now be at ten teams. Manchester Phoenix were back this time playing at Altrincham. Also the Hull Stingrays came on board. The league decided to enforce the 'playing rules', i.e. zero tolerance towards minor infringements. This was supposed to be in line with other leagues. Well I recall an early season home game against the Bison which descended into a farce. There were that many penalties being called there was little and no game flow. Eventually even the Panthers fans started booing at a Bison penalty call. Thankfully after a few weeks it all settled down.

Neil Black turned to Mike Ellis as his new coach. New players were added. Sean McAslan who became top scorer,

Corey Neilson and Danny Meyers. A certain Dan Tessier returned to Britain but only to join arch rivals the Sheffield Steelers. He showed what the Panthers missed though by finishing the league's top points scorer with 100.

The Panthers played in Europe again (Rouen). Their form was poor in France and continued in the League where they finished fifth. Coventry Blaze won the league and Challenge Cup. However, the Panthers season did end in triumph when they won the play-off title beating the Cardiff Devils on penalties at the NIC. Strangely the day before the Panthers also won on penalties against Belfast to advance to the final. The hero of the hour was netminder Rastislav Rovnianek (Rasto) who made excellent stops over the two games. Late addition to the side, Trevor Gallant, also played his part.

During that period it was the Coventry Blaze who were the standout team. Trevor Koenig was now in goal and their excellent trio of Neal Martin, Adam Calder and Dan Carlson used to dominate games. Head coach was Paul Thompson who did an exceptional job with a small club. The Blaze went on to win two more league titles (2007/08 and 2009/10).

Following Panthers play-off success they went on to win the Challenge Cup (2007/08). However they were still not in the frame when it came to the main trophy, the Elite League title. Mike Ellis paid the price and Corey Neilson was installed as player coach. His first move was to secure the return of Dan Tessier and sure enough his stats were as good as ever. He was backed up by other players who produced well during the 2008/09 season. Jade Galbraith and Brendan Cook being the standouts. No silverware was won though as the Steelers secured the double.

Season 2009/10. It was becoming quite predictable now for the Nottingham Panthers. It did not seem to matter which players came and went. Third place in the league seemed to be the norm, but when it came to the cup competitions it was a different situation. The Challenge Cup was rarely seen outside of Nottingham. I thought Neilson had certainly made some improvements and was starting to get his recruitment right with players like Brandon Benedict, Matt Francis and Jordan Fox. For me though I always thought he would need to find a more solid defence for the league season of over 50 games. The idea of we can score more than you will not always work. I also believe you need to play with four lines. Over the years the team have enjoyed some great wins at home on a Saturday night but not been able to back it up the following day. You need to have faith in all the players (just my opinion of course).

Season 2012/13. At long last the Nottingham Panthers became League Champions. Corey Neilson got everything spot on. He firstly made a tough decision to release Danny Meyers. I think this was mainly to allow him to bring in Jonathan Weaver. Neilson himself would then be behind the bench. I don't believe Meyers had done anything wrong but with the emergence of Steve Lee it may have been partly to do with the budget. Also experienced import defencemen were added to complete the back line in front of Craig Kowalski. The tipping point though was bringing in David Ling and Bruce Graham who scored a combined 78 goals, and using Jordan Fox as a two-way player was the icing on the cake.

Panthers won 42 of their 52 league games. They went on to complete the treble in dramatic fashion, Fox netting an overtime winner to see off the Giants 3-2 in the play-off final, Clarke and Werner with the assists. That season it was just meant to be! Cue amazing celebrations by the fans and players alike and why not? The success of 1956 was a long time ago.

Season 2013/14, and it was always going to be difficult to top a great season like the Panthers had. Some players moved on, Ling, Graham, Fox and Lepine all departed which left quite a gap. The team played in two rounds of the Continental Cup but injuries would take their toll overall. Even so they did stage an incredible comeback against Belfast (2-5 down) to retain the Challenge Cup on penalties. It was Paul Adey who would ultimately return to the Elite League as coach of the Giants who won the league title by a massive margin. Adey had enjoyed some excellent success coaching in Italy and Switzerland, so winning the league came as no surprise. What did shock me though was the Giants did not retain his services for the 2014/15 season. Strange things happen in sport!

So, to come right up to date for me, season 2014/15 is complete. Panthers played in the Champions Hockey League (CHL). The rest of the campaign though is best forgotten. Recruitment seemed odd. Too many players were similar, the team lacked flair, speed and even a bit of steel. Admittedly injuries again would play a part. The Steelers won the title when really the Braehead Clan should have closed it out. For the first time in some years the Coventry Blaze won the play-offs. In fact all the trophies were shared around when the Devils won the Challenge Cup (now played as a one-off final).

In all the years I have watched ice hockey in Nottingham one thing, or to be precise one person, has remained the same: the rink announcer Stef (David Litchfield). He has stayed professional at all times, a terrific achievement when you consider all the altercations including bench clearances and brawls on the ice. He remains calm and collected, pronouncing foreign names, ignoring the loud music and staying neutral with his announcements. If he had a shirt number it would definitely be retired when he hangs up the mic (hopefully not for some time yet!).

Writing these sections on the Nottingham Panthers one thing really stands out, and that is just how many different players have come and gone. Perhaps there is some food for thought there. A little more stability might result in a little more consistency.

Corey Neilson/Rick Strachan will return for season 2015/16. As always we look forward to it with much anticipation, after all, just where else would you want to be on a Saturday night?

Unfortunately we will not be watching the Hull Stingrays who went into liquidation in June 2015. The Elite League will stay at ten teams with the addition and return of the Manchester Storm. Interesting times, as always, lay ahead.

CHAPTER 4

CONTINENTAL CUP

This is a club competition for teams from around Europe who have finished league champions or play-off champions at the end of the previous season; the format has changed somewhat over the years. There are several rounds of the competition usually played at a selected venue which takes place over a long weekend. Four teams are involved with only the group winner advancing to the latter stages.

I have been attending this event for the past 12 years to see how successful the British clubs would be. It has been most enjoyable and it certainly gets you to places you would not normally visit. I find this to be quite refreshing compared to the normal tourist destinations.

LUGANO 2003

During the 2002/03 campaign the Belfast Giants represented Great Britain. At that time they played in the Ice Hockey Super League (ISL). The Giants hosted one of the early rounds in Belfast and finished group winners having triumphed over Rouen (France) 8-0, EHC Linz (Austria) 5-3 and Valerenga (Norway) 5-1 to make it to the final stage.

This was the first time I had travelled to see a European club competition. it was held during the early part of the year in Lugano, Switzerland, which is quite an affluent place with more than the odd fur coat around. A flight to Milan followed by a 90-minute train ride puts you in Lugano. It is a fairly easy journey except the train I caught was a Pendolino, one of those trains that seem to sway from side to side on corners. I think we tried one similar in the UK called APT. Anyway, it made me feel quite sick and I had to stand by a window for the latter part of the journey (I know, how pathetic).

I stayed at a hotel just on the edge of the town with a scenic view of the lake. The arena though was a good bus ride from the centre. Fortunately special buses were provided for all the games. It was always going to be a tough tournament for Belfast who deserved credit for reaching the final stage. It did not help when they had to play their first game against the hosts H C Lugano. There was a crowd of over 4,000 including several hundred from Belfast who made themselves heard giving great backing to their team.

Despite a good performance on the night the Giants lost the game 2-0. Playing centre for the Swiss side was the excellent Corey Millen. He is only 5 feet 7ins tall but he controlled everything when he was on the ice. I had seen him before playing in the DEL for the Cologne Sharks. He did ice in his earlier career for five NHL clubs. Shots on goal during the game were fairly even and to be honest I think the Giants were a little unlucky to lose the game. The local press though focused more on the style of hockey they played describing it as brutal and physical. It had all seemed rather tame to me.

The next game would see the Giants up against another Swiss powerhouse HC Davos with Jonas Hiller in goal. This time though the Northern Irish side drew much praise from the media with a top-class performance, winning the game 4-2, goals shared between Bowen, Karlander, Ward and MacDonald. Ryan Bach was in goal and the Giants had other top players on display like Sandrock (who re-joined the club some years later), Matsos, Kelman, Schulte, Stewart and Kruse to name just a few. Dave Whistle was the coach.

Later that evening I joined a bar full of Irish fans to celebrate their win. Actually I was not terribly discreet and walked in with a Panthers shirt on. It was like a scene from the wild west where everyone goes quiet and turns to look at you. Anyway, I was told I was very welcome but my team was not. It seems they all held a grudge over an incident at the Odyssey when their hero Paxton Schulte was flattened one evening by one of the Panthers players. I quickly glossed over that and heaped much praise on their team for the excellent performances so far in the competition. It was a really enjoyable evening.

I would not see the Giants again in the tournament as they went to play their next game in Milan who were co-hosting the event with Lugano. They lost a tight game with Bratislava 4-3 but finished a very creditable sixth in the tournament. I stayed in Lugano to see both semi-finals, the bronze medal game (which was actually won by Lugano), and the final which was between Jokerit (Finland) and Locomotiv Yaroslavi (Russia). Due to the hosts not making the final only 2,000 were in attendance. Now far be it for me to criticise the IIHF but this game was on a Sunday night and did not start until 8.30pm, and after several periods of overtime it was well past midnight when the Swiss fans vented their feelings at Rene Fassel (IIHF Chairman). I left before the end leaving just a handful of fans still in the building. The game had been locked at 1-1 for what seemed like forever. The Finns (apparently) won the Continental Cup 1-0 on penalties. I really do not get these late starts for games in Europe. I arrived back at my hotel after 1.30am. It was, overall though, a most enjoyable tournament. Lugano is a great place with welcoming fans so what more can you ask for? Except then I had to tackle that train again…

AMIENS 2004

During October 2004 the Continental Cup was held in Amiens, France. I managed to get a flight from East Midlands to Paris. It is then a 120k train ride north. Amiens is in the Picardy region of France. Captured by the Germans in 1940 during World War Two it was then occupied until 1944. There is much history there and in the surrounding areas which played a large part during that war.

My visit was to see the Nottingham Panthers play in Europe for the first time. These were the early years of the newly formed Elite League, which of course was a lesser standard than the Super League. Unfortunately the ISL was not viable long term due to finance. I was therefore expecting a difficult tournament for the Panthers who would be attempting to reach the latter stages of the competition. Standing in their way were the Milan Vipers (Italy), HDD Olympia Ljubljana (Slovenia) and hosts Amiens Les Gothiques.

During my train journey from Paris I spoke briefly to a very pleasant Canadian lady who I actually met again during the tournament at the arena. It turned out she was the wife of Daniel Tkaczuk, one of the Milan forwards. She told me she was still working in Canada so only came over to join Daniel when she could. The fans in Milan used to make her laugh as they completely ignored the smoking ban at their arena even though most of it was made of wood. Daniel Tkaczuk would only play 12 games in the NHL, but he did join the Nottingham Panthers

(2010/11). Sadly injury would limit his appearances and eventually he would have to retire from the sport.

I booked in at the Holiday Inn Express close to the station; it is roughly 15 minutes' walk to the arena (Coliseum). It is all part of a sporting club; there are two ice rinks and an Olympic size swimming pool all of which was council owned I was informed. The ice hockey rink holds just short of 3,000. It is small but a smart place with good viewing areas and a nice atmosphere also. The first game was the Milan Vipers against the Nottingham Panthers.

During breakfast at the hotel I discovered the Milan team was also staying there and they decided to hold a team meeting in earshot of myself. I tried to look invisible while staring at my croissant. I even had to eat more in order to look disinterested in their conversation. However, after my third croissant, it had become obvious so I had to leave. The main topic had been who would take out the Panthers' John Craighead as they could not risk him pushing their team around. Step forward Milan hard case Matt Smith (actually born in Kent). "It is my job," he announced. I was eagerly looking forward to this game already.

I strolled across town towards the arena. Amiens is quite lively with many shops. Several hundred Panthers fans were arriving and it was building up into a good atmosphere, however, my attention was drawn towards a minibus which pulled up near the arena. It looked like 'how many people could you fit into a mini'! More than a few Italians got out but it seemed like there were even more flags than people. It was standard dress, dark jeans and sunglasses, and the flags had the usual 'Ultras' displayed. Security at the rink seemed to always be evident in their section, but to be fair they seemed to support their team well and mixed with the other fans.

The game proved to be as tough as I had thought. Milan Vipers had won Serie A four times in succession and paraded a number of experienced players, in particular Niklas Sundstrom (749 NHL games) in his career and Craig Adams (829 NHL games) in his career. Other top players would include Mark Savard and Giuseppe Busillo who played for the Manchester Storm in the ISL (2001/02).

During that period the Panthers were coached by club legend Paul Adey. He set his team up well and they twice took the lead during the game but it finished 2-2 in regulation. Curtis Cruickshank was outstanding in goal, Kalmikov and Ahlroos scored the Panthers goals and the fight was as expected Smith and Craighead went at it, however, under IIHF rules both were ejected from the game. IIHF rules mean fighting is not just a five-minute penalty in this competition. So on to penalty shots at the end of the game. Panthers won 3-2, an excellent win, but wait… later during that evening Mick Holland (former Ice Hockey correspondent for the *Nottingham Evening Post*) joined fans in a local bar and informed us the penalty shoot-out win would only come into effect should both teams have equal points/goal difference at the end of the tournament prompting another rant by me at the IIHF. The evening game was a straightforward 3-0 win by Amiens against Ljubljana.

The second morning of the tournament and a quiet breakfast. No Milan meeting that day. I must have been rumbled. I was then joined in Amiens by friends who had made the trip by car, but unfortunately they missed the first day of the tournament due to work commitments.

The early game on the Saturday would see the Panthers squeeze out a 1-0 win over Ljubljana. This was a tight game and it would leave the Panthers with mounting injury problems. David Clarke and Paul Moran continued to play despite injury but Jan Magdosko would take no part and Roman Tvrdon ended up being taken to hospital during the first game. He was ruled out for the rest of the tournament.

The evening game would see Milan defeat the hosts Amiens 4-0 in a display of power. Icing for the French club was former Sheffield Steeler Timo Willman. Nottingham Panthers hopes of progressing in the tournament were all but gone, when in their final game Milan beat Ljubljana 9-2. The Slovenia side played their backup netminder which angered the Panthers organisation.

The hosts Amiens faced off against the Panthers on the final evening, It emerged that the Panthers would need to win 12-0 to go through. It was an excellent atmosphere and both sets of fans played their part. Kalmikov and a brace by Craighead would defeat the French side 3-1. I thought the Panthers had been a credit to the Elite League. Despite the injuries it was a terrific effort but Milan would go through on goal difference. It was a pleasure to meet other Panthers fans in a bar after the final game and a big thanks to the players who came in to show their appreciation. It was a very good tournament but again I questioned the IIHF with their rules and I was not alone in this.

GRENOBLE 2005

This tournament provided me with an opportunity to travel to a part of France I had not ventured to before. Grenoble is in the southeast area at the foot of the French Alps in the Rhone-Alpes region. I took a flight to Lyon and a coach on to Grenoble. I booked in at a Best Western Hotel right in the centre of town and was joined by my friend Roy who is a well-travelled Blaze fan from Birmingham.

It was indeed the Coventry Blaze who were representing the British Elite League after winning the 'Grand Slam' the previous season. Ashley Tait scored the overtime winner against the Nottingham Panthers in the play-off final. Unfortunately, Paul Thompson (Blaze Coach) would lose many of his star players from that all-conquering side, Jody Lehman, Adam Calder, Dan Carlson and Andre Payette had all departed. I think to be honest this tournament had come at a bad time with Thompson trying to re-build his squad.

Amstel Tijgers (Holland), Herning Blue Fox (Denmark) and Bruleurs De Loups, Grenoble (France) would be the opposition with only the group winners advancing to the final stages. The arena was a short tram ride from the centre; the Blaze fans had come in numbers and created a really good atmosphere during the weekend. The opening game was Coventry against Herning. It proved to be a tight match throughout ending in a 2-2 draw. Cowley and Hutchings scoring for the Blaze who had

Martin Klempa in goal. Penalty problems hit Coventry during the game and they would have to improve on that if they wanted to progress. The evening game between Grenoble and Amstel would also end all square at 2-2.

Going into Saturday's games, a win for the Blaze was vital against the Amsterdam side who were icing their Dutch international star Tommie Hartogs. He actually played for Grenoble back in 1997. He was a vastly experienced ice hockey player in Europe with 239 appearances in the DEL and also appearing for his country Holland in 15 World Championships.

This game though was a strange one with all the goals coming in the first two periods. The Blaze built up a 4-0 lead with goals from Moore, Cowley and Poirier (2). It was all plain sailing but Amstel hit back with four unanswered goals to level the game. Fortunately for the Blaze it was Joel Poirier's day when he completed his hat trick to notch the winning goal. Coventry closed out the game in the final period and they needed their experienced players to pull them through which included Ashley Tait, Mark Lefebvre, Graham Belak and the excellent Neal Martin, who, in my opinion, is one of the best defencemen to have played in the British League during his spells with the London Knights and Coventry Blaze. The evening game would see the hosts triumph over the Danish side 3-1 and therefore set up a winner takes all contest in the final game on the Sunday, Grenoble v Coventry.

An enthusiastic crowd of just under 3,000 would see Grenoble get on top early in the game. The French were a fast skating side with good stickhandling and passing skills. The Blaze found it tough going and would again be on the wrong side of the referee. Grenoble were smart and played on this to their advantage at the time, provoking the English side. The Blaze fell behind 2-0 conceding goals in the 22nd and 32nd minutes. Actually it could have been worse if Klempa had not saved a penalty shot.

The game would unfortunately get out of hand in the last period when the Blaze just lost it when they tried to get back in the game. They were given 19 penalties totaling 67 minutes, but to be fair they did anger the local crowd by trying to start something in order to change the game. Despite some late pressure though the score did not alter and Grenoble went forward in the Continental Cup. The Blaze fans were unhappy with the officials but with all my experience of watching our North American style of ice hockey in Europe this was nothing new. I think overall it came down to being a few players short up front. Where were Calder and Carlson when the Blaze needed them?

ROUEN 2006

It was to be a third visit to France in as many years, this time to Rouen in the northwestern area of France, which is the capital of Normandy. The city is famous for the execution of Joan of Arc in 1431. Claude Monet painted the Rouen Cathedral which was valued at $40 million. A flight to Paris followed by a 75-minute train ride put me in Rouen to see the Nottingham Panthers second attempt in this European competition.

Mike Ellis was the coach for this venture and they were up against the hosts Rouen Dragons, Salzburg Red Bulls from Austria and the Danish side Sonderjyske. The Nottingham Panthers fans travelled in numbers again and provided excellent support throughout the weekend along with the French and Danish fans. Sadly, not one Austrian was in attendance prompting a chant of 'You've got no fans' to the Salzburg team.

Having booked into my hotel near to the station, I joined a group of friends for a pre-match drink. I must say a big thank you to the staff at the Rouen arena who sorted out our tickets. Their GM was actually Canadian; all were very helpful and welcoming.

The first game was Salzburg against Sonderjykske and it was a very even game with both sides exchanging goals. The main threat for the Austrians were Thomas Koch and Dieter Kalt. It ended 4-4 after overtime with the Red Bulls claiming a penalty shoot-out win. So on to the Panthers opening game against the hosts and it did not go well. Rouen exploited the penalty problems the Panthers ran into (sounds familiar). The French side scored three power play goals and converted another on a four on four situation. Neilson and Krajicek did reply for the British side but it ended in a 6-2 defeat.

Yet again I was joined by friends the following day who had come over by car, and guess what? They missed the first day of the tournament again due to work commitments. How could work be more important than ice hockey?

Unfortunately, things would not improve against Salzburg during the early game on the Saturday. The Panthers would concede more power play goals in a 5-2 defeat to the Austrians, James Cooke and Rod Stevens with the consolation goals. It was already clear the Panthers were struggling in this tournament; we did not see the same fight and commitment as we had in Amiens.

The final game on the Sunday ended with another defeat this time to the Danish side 4-2, Geoff Woolhouse replacing Evan Lindsay in goal, Clarke and McAslan (who was later thrown out) scored the goals. The tournament provided few positives for the team, which at times looked jaded and slow; too many penalties would again prove decisive in each game. Salzburg overpowered Rouen 6-0 in the final game and would progress to the next phase of the competition. The Panthers fans had been excellent all weekend and even had the Austrians thanking them at the end of the tournament for creating such a great atmosphere.

A Monday morning stroll along the river Seine in lovely sunshine gave me time to reflect on the Panthers performance. I then took the train to Paris on the way home and sat outside at a Parisian café with a nice glass of wine. Unfortunately my thoughts on the overall performance failed to improve. Coach Mike Ellis declared himself unhappy also and it was not long before some players were released including Evan Lindsay and Blaz Emersic.

BOLZANO 2009

This trip was to be a nostalgic return to the north of Italy to Bolzano. I had spent a week there in 1994 to watch Great Britain play in Pool A of the World Championships, and it is a really attractive area to visit, so myself and Karen decided to make a little tour. A few days in Venice and a brief trip to Verona before taking the train to Bolzano.

It was late November and the town was just opening its Christmas market. We stayed at the same hotel in the centre as I had done in 1994; very little seemed to have changed. The tournament was in the final group stage so a place in the January super-final was at stake. The Sheffield Steelers were the British representatives, and HYS Hague (Holland) and HDK Maribor (Slovenia) joined the hosts Bolzano Foxes to complete the competition line up.

The arena is quite a walk from the town so we caught a local bus to be at the first game which was the Sheffield Steelers against HYS Hague, and it turned out to be an awkward game for the Yorkshire side. Dave Matsos was the coach and he encountered injury problems before the tournament and even needed to sign a replacement in goal when Andrew Verner joined in place of Kevin Reiter. The Steelers showed good determination throughout the contest which would see them take the points with a 4-3 win. Legue and Talbot were amongst the goal scorers. There was good support from the Steelers fans who had travelled. The second game would see the hosts Bolzano beat the Slovenian side 4-2.

Saturday would start at the Christmas market before a visit to the Café Metz. This was the post-match venue for fans and players back in 94, then on to the afternoon's game and it was a dramatic encounter between Sheffield and Maribor. Both teams matched each other goal for goal during the game but grit and determination would see the Steelers through winning 5-4 with a hat trick from Matt Hubbauer and a brace from Brad Cruikshank. Fortunately for the Steelers they were not taking too many penalties in the tournament; this would have taken its toll with a short bench. The Italians triumphed again 3-0 against the Hague in the late game, so it would, as expected, all come down to Sunday evening's final game.

It would again be another late start for a game on a Sunday night. The arena is quite big for Italian ice hockey with a capacity of over 7,000, but tonight's attendance is 4,300 with the usual ultras roaring their team on. My concerns that evening for the Steelers would be how they would manage their fitness with three games in as many days. I mentioned the injury problems and it is a major blow to be without the likes of Scott Basiuk and Rod Sarich.

The game started amongst a lively atmosphere and it was not long before the locals were in shock when Dowd and Talbot put the Steelers into an early two-goal lead. In goal for the Foxes was Pasi Hakkinen; the Finn played briefly for the Nottingham Panthers in the 2001/02 season. The fast skating Italians though would hit back to lead 3-2 by the halfway mark with goals coming from their Canadian trio of Jardine, Claire and Corupe. This was a pulsating affair and Joey Talbot was to level for the

Steelers leaving the game locked at 3-3 in regulation. I thought Brad Cruikshank did well during the game to curb his abrasive style as both teams would take equal penalties in the game.

Overtime would not produce a winner so a shoot-out was necessary with the Steelers Matt Hubbauer becoming the hero with the winning goal to send the Steelers into the final. It had been a top effort from the British side. I must pick out a very young Robert Farmer who looked an excellent prospect with his performance over that weekend. I think also much praise should be heaped on Dave Matsos as he and his team had to dig deep to advance to the final. So guess what, with the late finish another problem finding transport and it was after midnight again when we returned to our hotel. I think Rene Fassel and myself need a word.

The Steelers went on to the Continental Cup final in January 2010 held in Grenoble, I did not make the trip but followed the scores with interest. It could not have been a better start for Sheffield beating the hosts 5-2 on their own ice. Unfortunately that was as good as it got as they went down to Minsk 1-4 and to the eventual winners Salzburg 1-6. The Steelers would finish third overall which was a very creditable performance by the British side.

LANDSHUT 2012

Nine years on from Lugano, the Belfast Giants would again be our representatives in the Continental Cup; this time, of course, it would be as a member of the Elite League. On this occasion we could only make it for the Saturday game of the weekend tournament, a game which was the potential decider between Landshut Cannibals and the Belfast Giants.

A flight to Munich and around a 50-mile southeast train ride puts you in the capital of Lower Bavaria. It is a 15-minute walk to the centre of town and our hotel. It was a grey afternoon but many people were sitting at outside bars and cafes so we joined them for a pre-match meal. The Giants fans had come in numbers and it was clear that they were a hit with the locals. It seemed extra supplies of beer had already been required at the arena. Unfortunately, there had not been the time to see the other two teams in the competition, Geleen Eaters (Holland) and HSC Csikszereda (Romania). The Giants had already beaten the Dutch side 11-1.

We strolled to the arena along the River Isan. These games are always reasonably priced, only 30 Euros for the whole tournament of six games. It was a fairly old rink with standing all down one side. The Giants and Cannibals fans were side by side and created a deafening racket.

Landshut play in the second league in Germany now known as the DEL2, financial constraints prevented them from being promoted to the top league I was informed.

Now I had seen the Cannibals play before so I knew they were a strong side in defence backed up by good goal tending. This proved to be a difficult game for the Giants. Very early in the contest though they had several chances to take the lead with Garside hitting a post. However, the Germans were excellent at drawing penalties and the Austrian referee was typical of the officials I have seen in Europe, penalising our style of hockey with some really soft calls.

The Cannibals took full advantage with Cody Thornton and Peter Abstreiter (2) scoring to put their team 3-0 ahead by the first break. If the referee had angered the Giants players and fans in the first period, then they would be positively incensed by him in the second when he ruled out a Fournier goal. Belfast needed to chase the game and that played into the Germans' hands with their counter-attacking being lethal as Stephen Murphy was left high and dry. Kronthaler and Trew made it 5-0 before Champagne did pull one back. The Giants looked jaded at this stage and Landshut would add two more through Davidek and Brandl to win 7-1.

The German fans were unhappy at the final buzzer as Phillips took a swing at one of their players, but he missed. That summed up the night for the Belfast Giants.

Back in the hotel bar I joined a group of Giants fans to discuss the game. Some were concerned other Elite League club fans would laugh at this result but I disagreed. Playing in Europe is a difficult task at the best of times. These teams have much higher budgets and the emphasis is put on fitness, stick handling, passing and defending. They are also very smart, they are aware of our bump and grind style and know referees do not like it, and they exploit it. This is just my opinion of course. Anyway I had to admit I was from Nottingham (a little more discreet this time), but nine years on and the Giants fans were still on at me about what happened to Paxton Schulte. My word, they really do have long memories. Interesting people though and a pleasure to talk hockey with them.

NOTTINGHAM 2013

One of the early rounds in this year's tournament was held in Nottingham UK. The Nottingham Panthers were chosen for the third time to represent the Elite League in the competition following their all-conquering season which included winning the league title for the first time since 1956. The other teams included the HYS Hague (Holland), Dynamo Riga Juniors (Latvia) and Bipolo Vitoria-Gasteiz (Spain) who were a late replacement for Viking Sport Tallinn (Estonia).

The competition got off to a good start on the Friday afternoon with an entertaining game between Riga Juniors and HYS Hague. Both teams traded early goals but the Latvians showed their extra class with four goals during the second period to kill the game. It was quite obvious even at this early stage that Riga would be the team to beat. Their young players were quick with good stick handling and were not afraid to mix it on the physical side. The Dutch side stood up well to them but ended up on the wrong end of an 8-3 scoreline. There were 72 minutes of penalties during the game.

The evening game would see the hosts Nottingham Panthers up against the Spanish side Vitoria-Gasteiz who were given a warm welcome by the Nottingham fans for stepping into the tournament at short notice. If you could award points for effort and enthusiasm then the Spanish would certainly have qualified. Not really being at this level did not stop them having a go and the local fans appreciated it. Murray put the Panthers into an early lead only for Sosa to level before the first break. Panthers stepped up a gear though as the game went on and relentless pressure saw goals from Ryan, Clarke (2) and Capraro. Two late goals by the Spanish side followed but the Panthers eased home 5-3.

Saturday's games started with the Spanish taking on the Latvians with the local fans cheering for the underdogs. Riga would find it difficult to shake off their willing opponents and by the 34th minute they had been held at 2-2. Again though it was the extra pressure and speed that would see Riga break out with five unanswered goals to win the game 7-2.

The Nottingham Panthers would now need to beat HYS Hague to set up a showdown on Sunday night against Riga. The game was a tight affair in the early stages, however, it was Panthers live wire forward Matt Francis who made the difference completing his hat trick on the night with a penalty shot goal. Despite two goals in reply by Worm for the Dutch side, the hosts ran out winners 7-3.

So on to Sunday, the deciding day, the early game now a dead rubber would see HYS Hague beat Vitoria-Gasteiz 5-3 and the fans showed their appreciation to both teams for the entertainment they provided over the three games.

There were 3,200 in attendance to witness the final game, Nottingham Panthers against Riga Juniors. In my opinion this was the best game played at the National Ice Stadium during the season. I think also we must not get confused with the title 'Juniors' in the Riga name; mainly younger players, yes, kids most certainly not, the fans that saw this game were left in no doubt about this fact. It was clear from the outset that the Latvians' game plan was to attempt to draw penalties from the Panthers by hitting hard and getting in the face of their opponents. The Polish referee had his work cut out on the evening.

Francis fired the Panthers ahead with a short-handed goal at 5.24 in the first period. It then started to kick off. The Panthers forwards Matt Ryan and Bob Wren were slammed into the boards behind the goal. Both reacted and the fights started with Wren, in particular, laying into his opponent. Unfortunately IIHF rules in this competition mean that if you fight you are thrown out. Coach Neilson was unhappy with his two players for allowing themselves to be drawn into this. My view was different; you just could not have let the opposition intimidate you for the whole game. They had to stand up and put a marker down, so Wren & Ryan (Panthers) and Skuratons & Begovs (Riga) were ejected. There were 112 penalty minutes in the first period.

Neilson was now, of course, concerned by his team's short bench against the fast skating Riga side, but his team, with the fans firmly behind them, dug deep and increased their lead with a David Clarke goal only to be pegged back by Siksna who reduced the arrears for the Latvians who had good support themselves in the crowd. It was a highly entertaining game. Penalties still flowed (130 in total for the match). Craig Kowalski in the Panthers goal stood firm in the final period making 35 saves during the game, and Leigh Salters would finally kill off Riga with a third goal in the 48th minute to give the Panthers a 3-1 win and a place in the final qualifying round to be played in Italy.

Credit must be given to the Riga side who certainly came to play. They had great skill, speed and enthusiasm, but I would query their coaching tactics. The whole tournament was excellent. I think this showed the Elite League in a good light and I would hope for other IIHF events to be staged in Great Britain.

ASIAGO 2013

So a trip to the mountains of Italy to see the Nottingham Panthers compete in the semi-final stage of the Continental Cup. The first challenge was to actually get there; it's a ski resort up a mountain with no rail link and few hotels. The small town of Asiago is over 1,000 metres above sea level.

We took a flight to Venice and spent a night there and had dinner overlooking the canal. Boy did it rain that night. The last time I saw rain like that was in Nagano. The following morning was bright and sunny as we headed to the station to catch a train to Bassano Del Grappa. Unfortunately we ran into a train inspector along the way. I had forgotten to stamp our tickets at the machine; this seems to be required throughout Europe and he charged us an excess fare of ten euros as a penalty despite the fact that I came clean and apologised. It's 'company rules' he said. I said welcome to Italy. We moved on and we hired a car in Bassano and drove up to Asiago. It was a winding road with a gradual climb and as we neared the outskirts of Asiago we encountered the first snowfall of the season. The hotel we booked in at was a few miles outside of the town, however, it was a lovely place and the staff were excellent.

After a late lunch we drove into Asiago and parked at the arena which was free of charge. After collecting our tickets we took a short stroll around the town. It's a small place but with plenty of shops and cafes; the town had to be rebuilt after World War One.

The first game would see the Nottingham Panthers face the Russian club Toros Neftekamsk. I was surprised to see so many Panthers fans in the building as we arrived. The rink holds around 2,000 but with not that many seats. Unfortunately Karen suffers from a bad back so I e-mailed the club to request reserved seats. I was most impressed by the service. Not only did we get very good seats, they even had stickers with our names on them for the whole tournament. The only problem was how cold it was, and it actually made Edinburgh's rink seem reasonable.

The first game was a tough start for the Nottingham Panthers and it did not help with the team being hit by injuries. First choice netminder Craig Kowalski had to be replaced by Neil Conway following an ankle injury sustained in a game against the Coventry Blaze. Bob Wren and Eric Werner were also out. In addition Rob Lachowicz pulled up early in the game against Toros and this would cut short his tournament. Roared on by an excellent contingent of Panthers fans, the team matched the tough, fast skating Russian side and by the end of the second period they were in front 3-2 with goals from Stevie Lee (2) and Matt Ryan. Unfortunately, some would say, as usual, penalties would cost the Panthers with Toros adding two power play goals in the third to win the game 4-3, their winner coming with less than two minutes left. Panthers were called for 42 minutes in penalties in total.

The evening game saw the hosts Asiago run out 3-1 winners against the Kazakhstan side Yertis Pavlodar who actually outshot the Italians 42-28. Devergio scored twice to seal the win.

Saturday provided us with the opportunity to view the area and see more of the town of Asiago. It was quite obvious this place would be full of skiers in the main winter season being at the foothills of the Italian Alps. That day though it seemed very quiet, hardly comparable to a Saturday afternoon in Nottingham. The main square was in the process, however, of setting up a Christmas market.

The first game would see the Nottingham Panthers again face off early. Yertis would provide stern opposition and it would be a backs against the wall display. Conway faced 42 shots and was excellent under some extreme pressure, and even though the Panthers managed only 19 shots on goal Loyns and Benedict would both convert to give the team a 2-1 win. The great fighting spirit reminded me of the team that played in Amiens in 2004.

Panthers had much bigger fans at the game. Having assessed the rink temperature from the previous day it was obvious that suddenly everyone had several layers on under their hockey shirts. Quite right too!

The late game saw the Italians put themselves in the box seat when they hit six against Toros winning 6-2 despite facing 47 shots; Borrelli scored a hat trick in front of more than 2000 fans. That night was the coldest of the weekend and it took a good 30 minutes to defrost the car before we could drive back to the hotel.

Sunday was the final day of the tournament. We arranged for the hotel manager to provide us with a taxi service to allow us to have a couple of pre-game drinks. We expected another quiet day in Asiago but how wrong could we have been. The Christmas market was in full swing and the whole town was packed with people and families out shopping and filling every bar and café available.

After a couple of purchases from the market we headed to the rink to see the early game between Toros and Yertis, and what an excellent game it was with both teams going for the win. In the end it was the Kazakhstan side who triumphed 4-2 and this left the final game between Asiago and Panthers as the decider. The Italians only needed a point to qualify for the final round, whereas the Panthers would have to win in regulation. We needed a couple of glasses of wines before this one.

So here we go, the place was heaving and the 'Kop End' was rocking for the game. The Panthers fans had moved to the far corner of the arena and did their very best to make themselves heard. Our reserved seats were right in the middle of the Asiago season ticket holders. It all remained friendly except for one irate Italian lady who reacted to Henley crushing one of her favourites on the boards. She ran to the front, gave the full finger and shouted, "Bastardo." A bemused Dan Green on the bench turned around in amazement. However, her team would hit back in a different way by taking a two-goal lead both on the power play.

David Clarke silenced the arena though with goals in the first and second periods to level the game only for Layne Ulmen to regain the lead for the hosts with yet another goal with a man advantage. The Hungarian and Swiss referees did not call Asiago for a single penalty until the third period, and even then they broke up the play with 'man in the crease call'. If you get on the wrong side of European referees you have no chance. The Italian coach John Parco (former Ayr Scottish Eagle) obviously knew how to exploit the situation.

Despite their fighting spirit Panthers were not able to find another goal and went down 3-2. In the last minute of play Chris Murray had enough of wind-up merchant Paul Zanette and threw him around like a rag doll. Cue the lady leaving her seat again. Both players were ejected. On reflection, I really would have liked the game to have flowed more and on even strength the Panthers, despite their injuries, may well have come out on top. Talking of injuries, Lynn Loyns fell heavily into the boards during the game and took no further part.

One surprise to me during the tournament was even with so many defenders out, I do not think Tom Norton got onto the ice during any of the games. The biggest surprise of all though was that oxygen was not brought out for Jon Weaver. The amount of ice time he had in three days was unreal and his face told the full story at the end I felt.

So, our taxi awaited and a few wines back at the hotel was required to allow a full debrief of the competition. Short-handed due to injuries proved too much for the team. Even allowing for their fighting spirit, too many power play opportunities for the opposition in two out of the three games was decisive. Player of the tournament for the Panthers, our choice, was Neil Conway who faced 99 shots in three days.

The following day we made our trip back in lovely sunshine. The train trip from Bassano to Venice started with me stamping our tickets prior to boarding...

HC Asiago, just a word on their trip to the final round played in Rouen, France. It started well enough with a stunning 6-0 win over the hosts, but after going down 5-1 to Donetsk they were also beaten by the surprise tournament winners, the Stavanger Oilers.

LAST WORD ON THE CONTINENTAL CUP

Having now been to many of these tournaments over the years, I think the British clubs have competed quite well against teams who play a different style of ice hockey based on stick handling, puck possession and speed with also more emphasis on defence. Our style of bump and grind and also dump and chase is foreign to most sides in Europe. These teams always seem to roll out four lines which we struggle to do with our lack of depth, in particular with our young British talent. In addition we seem to get on the wrong side of the officials far too often in games. Unfortunately, for some years we have had a reputation for this and quite honestly I feel this leads to some extremely soft calls.

CHAPTER 5

WINTER OLYMPICS

An opportunity to watch ice hockey at the 1998 Winter Olympics in Nagano, Japan was not to be passed up. Planning would be key to this being a successful trip. Sometimes though even the best research can still not guarantee that you will make the right choices. Three of us travelled but with only myself being an avid ice hockey fan. We needed to obtain tickets quickly for the games otherwise it would not be worth the risk of travelling, so an application was made well in advance to Sportsworld Travel in Oxford.

Individual security checks were required before you were allowed the opportunity to purchase tickets and I found this company to be very efficient. All this took time but we eventually got the tickets we wanted, two top games from the group stages which were Russia v Finland and USA v Canada. Prices though were very high at £75 per game and this was 17 years ago, so I cannot imagine what the 2014 games in Sochi cost.

Anyway, delighted at having tickets to a world event, accommodation was the next target. Unfortunately,

Nagano is not that big and when the world's media/ TV crews have been housed along with competitors and officials, the rest of us were left to travel from as far away as Tokyo or Kyoto which is two and a half to three hours by train. Fortunately, the Bullet Train (Shinkansen in Japanese) was excellent and coupled with a rail pass we purchased it gave us so many options. We stayed for a week in Japan and based ourselves in Tokyo and Kyoto; this allowed us to visit Osaka and Hiroshima. Other events at the Olympics though were not considered as venues, and travel and cost were not good so ice hockey was the only Olympic sport we attended.

Flights were easily booked with Lufthansa from Birmingham via Frankfurt although the main flights to Tokyo were totally full which made for a cramped eleven-hour flight in economy. Japan was great with friendly people who were only too pleased to help. The transport system was excellent and the winter climate there was not that bad really, wet rather than cold.

Nagano is a busy place with plenty of restaurants and shops. The arena was a good 30 minutes' walk from the station and it was smaller than I expected for such major games but good for viewing. We were positioned behind the goal, and although it was a good seat for £75 I expected centre ice. The first trip to Nagano was to see Russia v Finland. We used our rail pass to book certain trains and seats on the day. We were advised to do this with so many people travelling from Tokyo. When we waited for the Bullet Train to pull in to the station you needed to stand as directed by your ticket. Numbers were highlighted on the floor and the train stops exactly where you have to get on as it would be nearest to your seat. The train was very comfortable, quiet and smooth, and you would never know you were travelling at high speed. The only problem was it was so hot on board.

Arriving in Nagano we realised we were at a world event. Everything was well organised and there were marquees everywhere with live TV screens showing everything that was happening. Helpers were on every corner to direct you to your event.

This was the first time the NHL had agreed to a mid-season break to allow all the players to be available for selection for their participating countries. Russia, however, were still missing some of their stars through injury. You would not have realised that though as this game was quite simply top class – speed and movement were evident on both sides. Russia edged the game 4-3 with goals from Pavel Bure and Alexei Yashin with two assists for Sergei Fedorov. The Finns replied with a goal from Saku Koivu and three assists for Teemu Selanne. Jari Kurri at nearly 38 also iced for the Finns.

Both teams would meet again in the semi-final, and it would be the Russians who would triumph again this time with a score of 7-4 with Pavel Bure scoring an incredible five goals in the game, and he would go on to finish the tournament as top scorer. Although Finland were well beaten in that game, they still finished third overall and claimed a bronze medal.

While we were in Tokyo we stayed in a quiet area called Harumi. Our hotel translated was 'The Grand' and it could not be faulted except breakfast seemed like dinner, so much food and all of it seemed to come with rice. I have to be honest I did struggle at times with the food in Japan but that is mostly down to me having a rather bland pallet. When we eventually checked out of the hotel a strange thing happened. We were actually given money back. There were puzzled looks all around until it was explained that since we had made the booking the exchange rate had improved in our favour. We were quite knocked back by the honesty of the hotel.

Our second trip to Nagano was to see USA v Canada. It was a quick turnaround for us as the first game was on Sunday afternoon and this game started at 1.45pm on the Monday. The game provided a real buzz around the town and many Canadians and Americans were there to see the game. Other events were taking place but on this day ice hockey took centre stage. Below I have listed the full roster for both teams. It really was quite impossible just to pick out certain players; all the players that came out on the ice seemed to be superstars of the game.

USA	CANADA
Tony Amonti	Rob Blake
Bryan Berard	Ray Bourque
Keith Carney	Rod Brind'Amour
Chris Chelios	Shayne Corson
Adam Deadmarsh	Eric Desjardins
Bill Guerin	Theoren Fleury
Derian Hatcher	Adam Foote
Kevin Hatcher	Wayne Gretzky
Jamie Langenbrunner	Trevor Linden
Brett Hull	Eric Lindros

Pat Lafontaine

John LeClair

Brian Leetch

Mike Modano

Joel Otto

Mike Richter

Jeremy Roenick

Mathieu Schneider

Gary Suter

Keith Tkachuk

J.Vanbiesbrouck

Doug Weight

Al MacInnis

Joe Niewendyk

Keith Primeau

Chris Pronger

Mark Recchi

Patrick Roy

Joe Sakic

Brendan Shanahan

Scott Stevens

Steve Yzerman

Rob Zamuner

The expectations were high for Canada; they were nailed on to win gold according to fans and media alike. Their line-up just oozed class and they soon had the USA on the back foot when Rob Zamuner forced the puck past the American netminder Mike Richter after taking a pass from Wayne Gretzky. Keith Primeau then added a brace before Joe Sakic made it 4-0 in the third period. There were just over five minutes remaining before Brett Hull broke Patrick Roy's attempted shutout with a goal. It was a terrific game. The USA though went on to lose two of their group games and would only finish joint fifth overall in the tournament.

Canada won their group to advance to the later stages scoring 12 goals in the process.

We returned for a night out in Tokyo. I felt safe and comfortable in the city and it was a very lively place. Finding a restaurant and bar could sometimes be a little confusing though when trying to read menus. Fortunately most places seemed to have window displays with plates of food you could choose from. After a good meal we decided on a stroll back to the hotel and stopped at a bar. We had to try a typical Japanese place but within minutes we were a little concerned. We ordered a couple of beers and I tried the Saki wine, then we were joined by three Japanese ladies. A little panic set in as first thoughts were these may be 'ladies of the evening', and secondly just how much were these drinks going to cost? Obviously we could not just leave, the last thing we wanted to do was insult the locals. We need not have worried as the bar turned out to be a hostess bar. These ladies sit and chat with you while topping up your drink at every opportunity, and prices were just normal for the area. My problem though was Saki. I still shudder now with just the thought of the taste. I had to move on to Kirin. The whole day had been a memorable one and thoroughly enjoyable.

The final part of our stay in Tokyo was to take the full day bus tour, highly recommended which provides you with a real insight into the past and present day. Following this we moved on to Kyoto for the final three days of our stay.

We purchased the rail pass prior to going to Japan. It represents excellent value and gives you the opportunity to visit just about anywhere in the country. Kyoto is fairly central so easy to go to places like Osaka that has an excellent castle. Our next destination though was Hiroshima. Now to be honest I was a little unsure about going, however, some years previously I had been in Hawaii and visited Pearl Harbour, so it was all about history.

We spent the best part of a day in Hiroshima visiting the town which made you feel like you were in the real areas of Japan. The Peace Memorial Park was a sombre place that made me feel really sad. The A-Bomb Museum tells the whole story. This was no ordinary museum it just paints a picture of destruction and the people of Hiroshima. This had been a different kind of experience!

Back in Kyoto I had been keeping a watch on the progress of the ice hockey at the Olympics. Watching two games and being part of the whole experience leaves you wanting more, and when the semi-final was announced between the Czech Republic and Canada I simply had to go and try and get into the game.

I went alone to Nagano and started the day at the Kyoto main station. I needed some breakfast but more noodles and rice seemed to be the only thing on offer. I decided to sit in a restaurant in the hope of seeing an English menu. No chance of that, but wait, a strange thing happened. A waitress came up and asked me if I would like cereals and toast. I could have kissed her.

Now unfortunately the train from Kyoto to Nagano is not the Shinkansen and as a consequence the journey took five hours. I was greeted with persistent rain on arrival so the walk to the arena was not pleasant. Outside the arena on our first trip we had been talking to one of the touts, a chap from London. They all seemed to be part of a syndicate. Anyway, he remembered me and I managed to buy a ticket from him at face value (£75).

This time it was centre ice next to the officials of Team Canada. You may guess where the tout got his ticket. There were two gentlemen next to me who were from Bradford but had lived in Toronto for some years and worked for the Canadian Hockey Association. It seemed though that all three of us had been in the same place before, a football play-off final at Wembley played in May 1996, Bradford City v Notts County (one best forgotten). A small world.

This game is still regarded as one of the best ice hockey games in recent times. The level of skill on the ice was mouthwatering. Defences backed up by netminders Hasek and Roy would dominate the game for the first two periods. In the third period the Canadians were rocked by a Czech goal scored by Jiri Siegr. Following this, waves of attacks would descend on Hasek's goal. It looked like the impossible would happen but with just 63 seconds left Trevor Linden found the equaliser.

Ten minutes of overtime followed without a winner so a penalty shoot-out of five per team would be needed. What followed would leave all of Canada in shock. Penalty shots were taken by Fleury, Bourque, Niewendyk, Lindros and Shanahan but none were able to get past Hasek. Meanwhile at the other end, Roy would stop four Czech penalties but Robert Richter was to score the only goal and put the Czechs into the final. I guess one of the mysteries of our time is why the 'great one', Wayne Gretzky, did not take a penalty shot. To this day Canadians prefer not to talk about that day in Japan.

It got worse for Canada when they lost to Finland 3-2 in the bronze medal game to finish a surprising fourth in the tournament. For the Czechs though it was to be complete elation when they secured Olympic Gold with a 1-0 win over Russia in the final. Dominik Hasek at this point must surely have been the best netminder in the world. Petr Svoboda scored the winner against Russia to become a national hero. Other great Czech players on the team were Martin Prochazka, Martin Rucinsky and probably their best player of all time, Jaromir Jagr.

For me, it had been a wonderful experience, one of those to look back on and say 'I was there'. However, should I have the occasion to be in the company of Canadian ice hockey fans I would most definitely avoid any mention of that day.

A side issue though was when a wife of a Canadian player was very annoyed that she was not offered a discount on some of the merchandise she bought, "I am the wife of a NHL player," she bellowed. The arena knew she was there and people looked at her in disgust. I walked away in disbelief. On the way back to the station I walked through what seemed like a monsoon. I have never seen rain like it. Along the way there were tents with free soup, tea and snacks and, having stopped to sample some soup and with water dripping from my cap, I turned around to find myself being interviewed on Nagano TV. When I gave the thumbs up and tried to say how welcomed I felt at the Olympics the Japanese crew went into raptures. Surely they did not think I was a player?

Our trip to Japan came to a close and it is one of the best trips I have ever been on for various different reasons and certainly left me with many great memories.

I have since seriously looked at attending another Winter Olympics in Turin (2006) and Vancouver (2010). Unfortunately both were simply 'out of reach'. Travel to the destinations was not an issue but sadly everything else was. Tickets for the ice hockey games were very difficult to obtain and the cost per game was astronomical. Accommodation was a major issue with very little available near to the cities (even if you could afford it) and no car hire available to get to the surrounding districts. None of it was user friendly so I really did not look past this, and for Sochi (2014) I did not even consider it. What a shame when ordinary fans are virtually pushed out by cost and availability. Hopefully though there will be another opportunity in the future.

For teams looking to reach the final stages of the Olympics outside of the top Pool A nations, qualification rounds are played over a period of time. I have been to watch three of these tournaments. Great Britain are ranked 22nd in the world so it is more than a difficult task to qualify. In fact they have not done so since 1948. However, it must never be forgotten that Great Britain won the Gold Medal in 1936 at the Winter Olympics staged in Germany in Garmisch-Partenkirchen (No, I was not there!).

The qualification for the 1998 Nagano Olympics started for Great Britain in 1996, drawn in a five-team group along with Slovenia, Denmark, Holland and Switzerland. It was an eight-game per team group comprising of home and away fixtures. The winner of the group would advance to the final qualifying stage. Great Britain did not lose a single game winning five and drawing three. The deciding match against Switzerland would be at the 'House of Steel' in Sheffield.

The Great Britain team at that time was coached by Peter Woods; quite a few dual-nationals made up the squad. The qualification campaign had gone really well with away wins in Ljubljana (5-4), Copenhagen (3-2), Heerenveen (8-2) and a draw in Lausanne (2-2). Unfortunately, the Swiss had more than matched the Great Britain results and led by one point going into the final game in Sheffield.

The teams traded goals with Tim Cranston (Sheffield) and Richard Little (Basingstoke) keeping the score level at 2-2 before Doug McEwan (Cardiff) put Great Britain in front. Unfortunately the Swiss would find the all deciding equalising goal with a shot that squeezed through the pads of Bill Morrison in goal for Great Britain. The game ended 3-3. The Swiss advanced but still failed to make the final 14 teams for Nagano when they lost 2-0 to Austria in a play-off decider.

Previously I had managed to see all the games in the pre-Olympic qualification for Lillehammer 1994. The games were part of a mini tournament also played in Sheffield. Great Britain was coached by Alex Dampier. It was to be a tough tournament. A tight 2-2 draw against Poland was creditable and this was followed by an even match against Japan, but an empty net goal would seal the win for the visitors. After this point Great Britain ran out of energy and ideas and were well beaten by Latvia 8-4 and eventual overall group winners Slovakia 7-1.

This was actually Slovakia's first appearance in the Olympics as an individual country. They went on to reach the quarter-finals at the main event in Lillehammer losing out to Russia by the odd goal.

My latest venture to see Great Britain in the Winter Olympic qualification would be to Riga, Latvia in 2013. This was ahead of the main event in Sochi, Russia in 2014. Great Britain had reached the final qualification stage by winning a four-team group in Nikko, Japan. They beat the hosts Japan 2-1 in the final match under the leadership of Tony Hand. I was disappointed not to be able to go back to Japan for the games so Riga was a must.

A direct Ryanair flight from East Midlands in early February put me in Riga before lunch on the opening day of the tournament. However, it seems I was quite fortunate with this particular flight. The plane had circled over Riga for some time before landing due to fog. It eventually touched down without a problem. Another flight though with other Great Britain fans on board flying in from London was refused landing and was diverted to Lithuania. From there it took some hours to get to Riga by road (not the best of trips apparently).

My hotel was right in the centre and a 30-minute walk to the arena although it seemed inexpensive by taxi. In addition there was a good bus service. The first game started late afternoon between France and Kazakhstan and it was the latter that would jump into a two-goal lead inside 11 minutes. The teams traded goals in the second period before the French scored a second at 57.42. Strangely they did not take their goaltender off for the extra forward to try and force overtime in the last minutes of the game and lost 3-2.

Icing for Kazakhstan was Dmitri Upper who just seems to have played forever, also Kevin Dallman a Canadian who is now a Kazakhstan citizen. He has played in the NHL and KHL and his uncle is Marty Dallman who is also a Canadian but played for Austria. The Nottingham Panthers fans will remember him icing 73 times for them in the Super League (1996–1998). The best known player on the French side was netminder Christopher Huet who played well over 200 games in the NHL for four different clubs. He was part of the Chicago Blackhawks Stanley Cup winning team in 2009/10.

On to the evening game and Great Britain would face hosts and favourites Latvia. The arena in Riga is two tiered with standing at one end where several drummers and the most vociferous fans would be. I had seen Latvian fans in Europe before and to say they are enthusiastic is a gross understatement. Housed in the upper tier were several hundred Great Britain fans that had made the trip. The game started at a frantic pace and immediate Latvian pressure led to the opening goal in just under three minutes. Great Britain hit back though with a well created goal by Robert Dowd. Over the years though whenever Great Britain plays in Europe, 'short-handed' has become the norm with referees not taking to their style of play. This game would be no different as Latvia took the lead later in the first period with a power play goal, one of three they would convert during the game. Craig Peacock added a second but a sixth goal with eight seconds left would give the hosts a 6-2 victory. Steve Lyle back in goal due to Stephen Murphy's injury faced 39 shots. Mathew Myers was ejected from the game for a 'checking from behind' penalty.

The Latvians are a good side and ranked much higher than Great Britain and were an established Pool

A nation. In this tournament they were captained by Sandis Ozolins, a vastly experienced player who played over 1,000 NHL games for six different teams and over 250 games in the KHL. The fans in Riga adored him. Great Britain did not have anything like that kind of talent in their side but certainly made up for that on the night with sheer effort. As usual they were well supported by the excellent Great Britain fans. A nice touch at the end was a drum roll accompanied by great applause for the Great Britain Barmy Army by the Latvian fans.

Day two would see the British side face off against France in the afternoon game. I took a stroll to the arena but snow and ice made the pavements difficult so I jumped into a taxi after a lunchtime glass of wine. The French were another Pool A nation and it showed at times. Great Britain played well though and were a little unlucky to find themselves 3-0 down by the 35th minute, two power play goals again conceded. Great Britain came right back in the last period with goals from Craig Peacock and Robert Lachowicz, however, a late French goal would complete a 4-2 win for them with Steve Lyle facing 34 shots.

The evening game paired the two Eastern European teams together and what a great match it was. Latvia came out flying and scored twice in the first three minutes, but by midway through the second period Kazakhstan had equalised. Latvia regained the lead though at the start of the third period. However, in the last minute with their goalkeeper pulled, Kazakhstan thought they had equalised. The Latvian fans were in a frenzy by now. I had a real close-up of the incident and during the scramble around Masalski's goal it looked to me like the puck hit the forward's skate which forced it over the line. After a long delay the referee ruled out the goal by video evidence – 'the puck was kicked in'. Cue uncontrolled celebrations by over 10,000 Latvians. One of the many Great Britain fans in attendance insisted the referee disallowed the goal on police advice, hmm… A 3-2 win left the hosts needing just one point against France to qualify for Sochi.

The following day was a break in the tournament so a chance to look more around the city. I engaged in a walking tour around the old town. Light snow was falling which provided the perfect ambience to the area with many churches and narrow streets. There was certainly a Russian feel about the architecture and skyline. There were museums which detail Riga's and Latvia's fascinating history, in particular the occupation periods. Today though it is becoming more of a tourist destination for weekend drinking parties and there are certainly many bars to accommodate this.

In the evening it was a walk to the KHL bar. Dynamo Riga play in the KHL and have their own sports bar in the city. There was a good selection of drinks and food available along with split screens showing sport from around the world. In addition there was a shop with ice hockey merchandise to purchase. That night though it was clear the Great Britain fans had taken over the bar and dance floor. It was good to meet fans from all over Britain.

Sunday was the last day and back to normal with ice hockey games to complete the tournament. It started at

1pm with a dead rubber. Great Britain played their final match against Kazakhstan who could not progress either. Ben Bowns played in goal for Great Britain and it was a nervy start for him conceding two goals in the first two minutes. Discipline problems followed with five straight Great Britain penalties and from one of these they conceded a third goal. Three games in four days had now taken its toll and Great Britain looked a very tired side and eventually lost the game 6-0, Bowns facing 42 shots. It was a difficult tournament for Great Britain facing three Pool A nations. There was no shortage of effort though and Steve Lyle was named Man of the Tournament for Great Britain and well deserved. He really should still be playing in the Elite League.

So it was on to 5pm and all of Latvia was watching. Their team required just one point to get to Sochi, but hold on. The French had the audacity to take a two-goal first period lead. A packed arena was in shock. A win for France would put them through. Latvia hit back to level early in the third period at 2-2. The French pulled their keeper (Huet) and surrounded the Latvian goal but they held on for the draw with their fans ecstatic. It came as a surprise when the teams still had to play overtime to finish the game which France won with 40 seconds left. I thought they deserved the win on the night but Latvia deserved to win the tournament and have the chance to play in Sochi.

I am still baffled at the decision by Dave Henderson (French coach) on why he did not pull Huet in the first game and attempt to tie/win the game. It could have made the difference against Kazakhstan.

After the game I walked back to the hotel via the KHL bar for a final drink on the trip. To my astonishment they had run out of wine claiming I had drunk it all the previous evening. Outrageous!

It was an early morning Air Baltic flight home via Amsterdam the following day and a time to reflect on a really good tournament with excellent hosts. It was a great shame that a good friend of mine (Roy) who had booked to come on the trip had to miss out. He had been rushed into hospital a few weeks before and had to undergo heart surgery. He is a top man and a great ice hockey fan (Blaze actually). Fortunately he is making a good recovery.

Pyeong Chang, South Korea, will host the 2018 Winter Olympics. One thing is for certain, it will be another tough road for Great Britain.

CHAPTER 6

WORLD CHAMPIONSHIPS

In 1993 Pool B (second tier) of the World Ice Hockey Championships was held in Eindhoven, Holland. I had little and no idea of what these games were about. The Great Britain ice hockey team were involved and it soon became clear they were doing rather well. In fact they won all seven of their games and were promoted to Pool A. The GB coach was Alex Dampier. The team was a mixture of British players and dual-nationals who qualified to play.

Great Britain would now play with the very best countries in the world in Pool A. This would be played over two weeks in April/May 1994. The venue was Bolzano, Italy. These championships are held annually in a different location; usually the only players missing are NHL players who are still involved in the Stanley Cup play-offs which carry on until June.

At that time of course there was less information readily available, no Internet or social media etc. I therefore paid a visit to Waterstones to view books, maps etc. and gain some knowledge of Italy. I had no idea where Bolzano was. I was determined to go and decided on a flight to Munich. From there a train trip through Austria into Northern Italy. Bolzano is in the South Tyrol. The scenery was spectacular on part of the train ride.

Bolzano seemed like a market town with plenty of shops, bars and restaurants. The Italians there always looked smartly dressed. I managed to book a hotel in the centre; also staying there were the team Canada players and officials. Canada was in the same group as GB along with Russia, Germany, Austria and Italy. The other six teams would play in Canazei with the later stages of the tournament taking place in Milan.

I purchased a GB shirt for the Championships. It certainly got me noticed, and some puzzled looks were followed by questions/observations. You only play football in England, surely! Walking through the town prior to the first game the German fans spotted a few others and myself. Cue an 'England football chant'. I was then ushered into a bar that they had already turned into a bierkeller. At first I was nervous as I have said before, "football fans at that time = trouble." No such thing the chant went up "we are all eishockey fans." A beer was promptly put in front of me. It was then 50 questions about ice hockey in the UK.

Now if most of Europe seemed totally unaware of British ice hockey, the coaching staff of Team Canada were already ahead. I was pinned in the hotel by several members including the coach who I believe at that time was George Kingston. They wanted to know why Paul Adey would not be playing. I confirmed injury had ruined his dream. Of course they already knew GB would not be anywhere near their class, but even so they still seemed to seek my opinion on everything ice hockey.

It was time to head to the arena. Buses were available every day from the town centre to the rink, which is around three to four miles outside of the town. It was always the same, the buses were full of mostly German fans singing away, that was until the bus would stop along the way to pick up a lone Austrian. He was decked out in his red colours and had more badges than you could count. Silence would descend on the bus and then the Germans would greet his arrival with more noise. He was not deterred as every day he would be at the same stop and receive the same greeting.

The first day at the arena angered the fans. Italian security and police had set up to deal with football supporters. Security men were searching some of the ladies, and this, as you would imagine, upset them and overall it just seemed like unnecessary heavy-handed tactics. I spoke to a member of the British press. On arrival he had been given a welcome pack to the tournament which included a very acceptable half bottle of Chianti. However, after stepping out of the arena after the first game he was promptly searched and his wine was removed, this despite his protests and press pass. Thankfully after the first day it all settled down without any more hassle. I think the organisers had caused the situation.

Quite a few fans were there from different clubs supporting GB. I had lunch and several drinks with some of them during the week. Lovely people, good hockey fans. The first game for GB was against Russia. They had power, strength and speed in reserve. The British side was three goals down within seven minutes of the start. It was going to be difficult to cope. Terry Kurtenbach did reduce the arrears however, in the end Russia ran out 12-3 winners. Patrick Scott and Kevin Conway scored the other GB goals.

I liked the arena. It had good viewing areas and had a capacity of around 6,500. I think the best game I watched at the tournament was Canada v Germany. It was a capacity crowd and what an atmosphere. The Canadians edged it 3-2 with a Shanahan hat trick.

Most evenings were spent with fellow hockey fans at Café Metz Bar. The Canadian players were given free Budweiser there. I managed to claim a couple despite looking nothing like a hockey player. Standing chatting to Steve Duchesne obviously helped.

The games came thick and fast. GB were struggling defensively. It was not down to any individuals or any of the netminders. Quite simply the other national teams were in a different class. Playing at a high tempo, these sides had great movement on and off the puck, and this was evident in all the games. Fitness also played a part. A 4-0 defeat to Germany was not a bad effort, but after that tiredness seemed to become a factor and they went down to Austria (0-10) and Italy (2-10). Icing for the Italians was Michael De Angelis who later had a short spell with the Panthers.

It was becoming difficult to watch now but against Team Canada everyone seemed a little more relaxed. A chance to play against the likes of Joe Sakic, Luc Robitaille and Paul Kariya to name just a few, it was a dream to some of the GB players. A crowd of over 6,000 was in attendance. Canada showed their class by almost scoring at will. They had much more physical presence than GB. I do not think I have ever seen anyone as big as Bobby Dollas. Canada cruised home but one of the biggest cheers of the night came when GB scored through Rick Brebant. They even added a second when Conway converted. It finished 8-2. That was the end of the tournament for me as I needed to get back to work.

GB would now have to play a relegation match against Norway who had finished bottom of the other group. I managed to watch it on TV. It was a tight game locked at 2-2 with the GB goals coming from Ian Cooper and Rick Fera. Relegation was confirmed though when they conceded three goals in the last eight minutes to lose 5-2

Canada went on to win the final in Milan beating Finland 2-1. For GB though this had been a tough experience and I have to say it proved just how far behind that level we were.

For me I had thoroughly enjoyed the whole championship and would look to attend others in the future.

It's now been over 20 years since Bolzano. In that time GB has never made it back to Pool A. Some would say thank goodness for that. Their task has not been made any easier with the emergence of other nations following country splits. Slovakia, Latvia, Belarus, Ukraine and Kazakhstan are some that are now members of the IIHF. In addition Denmark and Switzerland have vastly improved. Even so, GB have come close on a couple of occasions.

My next venture was in 1997 to Finland (Pool A). I watched a few games at the Hartwell Arena – an impressive facility on the edge of the city. I also went by train to Turku, the second venue. It is an arena with the steepest terrace/seats I have come across. Good view though.

The next year was Basel in Switzerland. This was a much smaller venue with standing behind each goal. This is normal in Europe and creates a top atmosphere. The second venue was Zurich (home of the Lions). To be honest this was a multi-purpose building. I do not think ice hockey fits in there with little and no atmosphere.

In 1999 it was GB again this time in Pool B. It was in Denmark. The arena there is small with many standing places. It is a bus ride from the centre of Copenhagen to Rodovre. GB made a decent start to the tournament and wins against Slovenia (2-1) and Kazakhstan (1-0) put the team in a good position. A 2-3 reverse to Germany was followed by more wins against Estonia, Poland and Hungary.

So, the final game was against the hosts, Denmark. I could only get a standing ticket behind the goal. It was a real end to end game. I thought GB had the edge but had to finish the final minutes of the game killing a 5 on 3 penalty. In the end they had to settle for a 5-5 draw. Steve Lyle having an excellent game in goal.

The top teams from each group would now play off in a four-team play-off held in Sheffield in November 1999. What a strange weekend it was. GB were held 0-0 by Latvia, then 2-2 by Ukraine, a win against Kazakhstan would then have been enough for GB to get promoted.

Leading 1-0 near the end the visitors pulled their net minder and Tony Hand sent the puck the length of the ice only to hit the outside of the post resulting in an icing call. Following the face-off their opponents got control of the puck and equalised with two seconds left, the game ending in a 1-1 draw.

The final game was Latvia v Ukraine. It finished 0-0 with few shots, few penalties and both teams advanced to Pool A. GB were desperately unlucky not to be promoted and having played ten games overall in the Pool B tournament they lost only once. I will keep my thoughts to myself about that 0-0 draw between Latvia and Ukraine.

GB would now have one final chance of promotion. A one-game shoot-out v Norway (again), a game played in Eindhoven, Holland. I had to go. There were hundreds of GB fans there, but it ended in disappointment – a 2-1 defeat. It was so tight it could have gone either way.

I have to mention the GB Supporters Club (GBSC). Set up in 1993/94, it is an excellent run organisation raising funds for the GB teams and arranging trips to all the tournaments. Much praise must be heaped on the committee who work tirelessly to make it work. There are some really top people involved.

In 2000 I felt a need to follow the team again to Poland (Katowice). I booked a hotel near the two rinks being used for the Pool B tournament. I could only spare around five days due to work. I then discovered the GBSC were all staying in Krakow. Strange, I thought, 50 miles to travel each day. I soon realised when I arrived in the town why this decision had been taken. I actually had a day out in Krakow which confirmed my thoughts. Large square, outside bars/cafes etc. This was quite the opposite of Katowice with its concrete blocks/flats and little to do. It seemed like a typical Eastern European old town. Even so, prices were fairly cheap for food, drink and match tickets.

GB made a slow start to the tournament. The first game was in the smaller rink; around 300 watched a see-saw game which GB were edged out 6-5 by Estonia. Injuries to two of the GB netminders did not help. I thought the team looked slow and unprepared to be honest.

Slovenia were up next and again GB were behind for most of the game. However, Steve Moria equalised late on to force a 3-3 draw. Game three was against the weaker Holland side who had been promoted from Pool C. Young Joe Watkins was now in goal and another young prospect was making his debut, David Clarke. GB were far too good for the Dutch. A line of Hand, Brebant and Adey should explain why it finished 9-0.

So, it was on to a Sunday night in Katowice. With 8,500 in attendance in the big arena, it was Poland v GB. The Poles had dispatched the Germans 6-2 the previous night. I loved this match. The Poles had their fans in raptures after taking the lead. GB stood up to them though big time. Defenceman Scott Young (2) and Steve Cooper with a real blast were amongst the scorers. Tony Hand was immense with one goal and three assists. He looked a class apart. Young Watkins faced 41 shots saving 37 to cap a great performance. GB won 6-4.

At the end of the game GB fans and German fans (who had stayed to watch) were asked to remain in the building. Polish police would arrive to escort both sets of fans back to the town and to their hotels or coaches. Apparently groups of Polish hooligans had gathered outside looking for a fight. Not very sporting!

GB next faced Denmark and got a shock going 3-0 down in just seven minutes. In addition they lost Scott Young to injury. Steve Moria completed a hat trick as GB fought back to win 5-4. Unfortunately I then had to leave with two games left. When GB beat Kazakhstan 3-1 it meant a win in the final game against Germany would put GB back in Pool A.

I managed to watch the game on the DSF satellite channel. The first period was scoreless. GB were then up against it, and with only four recognised defenders left fit the Germans used their speed to apply pressure going 2-0 up. I thought both goals had an element of luck. However, in the third period it all went south. Mike Bishop was called for a high stick after a German player lost several teeth and that was it. The final score was 5-0, a little harsh but if you think back to those two opening games, well, they proved very costly in the end.

I did really enjoy the tournament, but perhaps visiting Pizza Hut four times was a bit much. Mind you, a large deep pan pizza for two, salad bar and garlic bread, washed down with a bottle of red cost £3 in total. Well, you just could not afford not to go again and again!

In 2001 I decided to visit Germany who were hosting Pool A. I really only had a long weekend so the first couple of days were spent in Hannover. A new arena had been built out of the city. Game tickets included local transport.

There were three of us that went and we decided to stay at the Radisson Hotel on the complex. Also staying there was the 'great one', Wayne Gretzky. It was quite strange as he just seemed to be everywhere we went, breakfast, bar, reception, you name it. Apart from a nod as he walked by I refused to bother him. I mean fans were even waiting outside the hotel to see him. I recall one such fan coming in on behalf of everyone to ask if he would sign autographs. He was a perfect gentleman, finished his drink and went out. I am not sure he ever got back in.

We managed to see Germany v Belarus but it was Canada v Russia that we looked forward to. It was not a disappointment. Canada won 5-1. Ryan Smyth was the Captain, with players like Kris Draper, Steve Sullivan, Joe Thornton and Roberto Luongo in goal. They were a strong side so it came as a surprise when they went out in the quarter-final. I managed to go to the second venue in Cologne for a couple of games. The Koln Arena is very similar to the MEN in Manchester. Just one stop on the train from the main station. It is certainly worth a visit.

The next few years I seemed to concentrate on Pool A. In 2002 I went to Sweden and attended games at all three venues: Gothenburg, which has quite a large arena, I even played roulette in the main railway station there, Jonkoping, which is a smaller venue with a good atmosphere, and it was the first time I saw Japan play there in the championships, and finally, Karlstad, a strange sort of place. My hotel was a former prison.

Latvian fans came in numbers to the tournament but found it difficult to get into bars due to their rather rowdy reputation. Also picture this – hand cream was given out to fans in between periods at the games!

Scandinavia was again my destination in 2003, Helsinki and Turku (Finland). Now if you have never been to a tournament involving Finland and their fans then you should experience it. The team are all ice hockey gods and drinking alcohol, well, the Finns take it to a different level. Old, young, male or female they are all the same, but what an atmosphere they create. At a game in Helsinki at the Hartwell arena, I bought a ticket from a Finnish gentleman outside. I was actually sitting next to him at the game, and when I arrived at my seat he had a beer and a pizza waiting for me. He would not allow me to buy a drink at the game. Great hospitality!

Eurosport TV used to cover most of the Pool A Championships for many years. I particularly enjoyed the commentary team Paul Ferguson and Richard Boprey. They were in tune with each other, had excellent knowledge of the game and players from around the world, good banter also, especially with the one-line comments. Shame they are not still involved today.

In 2004 Oslo, Norway, hosted Pool B. It was time to check in again on Great Britain. It was a short trip for me but still a chance to see some games. Chris McSorley was the GB coach. The team now had much younger players while still maintaining a level of experience.

It was tough going though with defeats to Hungary (3-5) and Holland (1-4) which was most disappointing. They did manage to hold the hosts Norway (4-4). I remember mostly the game against Belarus. They were a strong side and were not averse to knocking a few of the GB players around. Brent Pope took exception to this when he floored one of the opposition – result, a match penalty and the end of his tournament. GB lost 5-4. Nice to see David Clarke and Paul Moran on the scoresheet. A final game was a 6-0 win against Belgium to ensure their Pool B status.

At the airport on the way back I had a nice conversation with Gary Moran (Panthers GM) and his wife. They had obviously been in Oslo to watch their son, Paul. Gary has often split opinions amongst the Panthers fans. His passion for the club though is quite unbelievable. I found him to be open, honest and quite frankly a pleasure to talk to. Sometimes I do feel that certain fans blame him for everything, which is unfair, although I would recommend (suggest) that he leave the mic duties to others.

Also in 2004, Prague in the Czech Republic hosted Pool A and I managed to get to both tournaments that year. The security at the championships in Prague was extremely tight. You needed to allow 15 minutes to get in at the bigger games. The arena was brand new and fans flocked to all the games.

Now I mentioned hospitality before. Well I had a day to remember at one game. It was a quarter-final, Sweden v Latvia. I arrived outside the arena as usual before the game looking to buy a ticket. I purchased one (well I tried to) from a Czech gentleman. He indicated to follow him. I realised something was not right when instead of the security we went into the main entrance via a red carpet. After catching the elevator we were shown into a box. Actually it was a suite, and what a suite. There was a free bar, a three-course lunch and plush seats outside to view the game. I thought I would be asked to leave at any point. Surely this was a mistake.

At the end of the second period I was ushered out of the suite. I thought they must have clicked I was an imposter, but no I was now taken on a tour of the boardroom. All the Czech corridors of power that operate ice hockey. I noticed a framed photo of the 1998 Olympic team in Japan. I wanted to tell everyone that I was there but English was not understood. At the end of the game (Sweden won 3-1) I just kept thanking everyone but I just got the same bemused look. It had been some day. How lucky I was to experience it.

I managed to catch three or four games in Vienna (Pool A) in 2005. It's a lovely city with many outdoor cafés and excellent restaurants. The arena though was like a large auditorium. It lacked any kind of atmosphere. I did not have time to get to the second venue in Innsbruck. Germany were surprisingly relegated and would therefore join GB in Amiens for Pool B in 2006.

For that tournament I really slipped up badly and failed to book in advance. I could only get a hotel in Abbeville, which was fine, but I kept missing the evening game. I did find a small hotel in Amiens after a few days but although they were lovely people my days of sharing a bathroom are gone. So after that I left my bag and credit card at the Best Western and each night they found me a room.

The atmosphere at all the games was excellent. GB were struggling though, losing games to Hungary and France by the odd goal. They were then taken apart by Germany (8-0) and after a 4-2 reverse to Japan they had to win their last game against Israel. Thankfully they did 12-0. This was probably the weakest GB side I had seen. I do not believe there were any dual nationals in the squad. Germany easily won the Group.

In 2007 Ljubljana, Slovenia, hosted Pool B. What a surprising place. Karen and I spent a few days there and in Lake Bled. It was most enjoyable.

With Paul Thompson in charge, GB enjoyed a better tournament opening with a 4-3 win against Japan. Even so, the side ran into trouble with defeats against Lithuania (2-3) and Hungary (2-4). They did put in a good display against the hosts Slovenia led by NHL star Anze Kopitar. It still ended in a 4-0 defeat. At the games it always made me laugh when the home fans were split into two sections with a line of security and police in between. These were fans from opposing club sides.

Tony Hand played his final GB game in Ljubljana against Romania. As usual he was dictating proceedings. I recall one defence splitting pass to Jon Weaver which led to a goal. GB won 6-1 and finished fourth. I have never quite worked out why GB did not get third spot and a bronze medal. Japan had the same number of points, had won fewer games, had an inferior goal difference and had lost to GB, but still finished third? At the airport on our return I had the immense pleasure of meeting Tony Hand. What a thrill it was, I had long admired him as a player on the ice. Karen and I spoke at length with him on many things ice hockey including his autobiography – top player and a real gentleman. Thanks for all the memories!

During 2008 I returned to watch Pool A. This time it was played outside of Europe in Halifax and Quebec City (Canada). We headed to Halifax in Nova Scotia. For the first time I thought game/groups of tickets were starting to get considerably more expensive. We still attended quite a few games including Canada v USA. Actually even when we did decide to watch one of the games in the fan area, the sponsors insisted we had complementary tickets.

The following year was in Bern, Switzerland and this most certainly confirmed my thoughts on ticket prices. I even took up this issue with an IIHF official. He insisted we had one of their badges. My thoughts and comments on the subject made to him, I would guess, would be filed away. Just to compound the issue, having paid to see one of the games a drunken Swiss fan spilt his pint of beer down my back. It was accidental, of course, but I was saturated. Thank goodness our hotel was across the street.

It was at this tournament that Germany finished in a relegation spot. However, that could not happen because they were hosting the following year. Austria and Denmark were not pleased and needed to play-off to try and stay up. It was a game played at lunchtime on a Monday in Kloten near Zurich. We caught the train up there to watch. I mean there are not many occasions when you can watch ice hockey on a Monday lunchtime. Even better the sponsors were having a wine tasting.

Around ten Austrian fans were there and in true fashion they sounded like 100. It was a small compact rink. Austria, led by Thomas Vanek, raced into a two-goal lead but slowly Denmark eased their way into the game and finally sealed the win with three goals in the third period (5-2). Austria were undeservedly relegated.

In 2010 we returned to Germany, and it started with games in Cologne before moving on to Mannheim. We purchased two tickets from a tout outside the Koln arena for a game involving Finland. Unfortunately two other fans came to sit in our seats. We all had identical tickets. We soon figured out that it was our tickets that were forged. The other two people had bought tickets in those seats for the whole tournament. We moved as there were spare seats. I guess this was happening quite a lot as the tickets were just ripped at the corner on entry and not scanned. It has made us much more wary of buying tickets from those kind of sellers. Despite this we did enjoy our time there.

Hungary (Pool B) would be our destination in 2013. Hot weather greeted us in Budapest as we followed GB again. Tony Hand was at the helm, continuing after their attempt at Olympic qualification in Latvia. Again no dual nationals seemed to be in the squad. Over 7,000 Hungarian fans roared their team on against GB who actually took an early lead. Hungary completed a 4-2 win in the end. I'm afraid this set the tone for a poor championship.

The team looked slow and tired as they went on to lose all their games to Kazakhstan (0-5), Italy (1-5), Japan (1-4) and finally Korea (1-4). I have always thought GB had a goal scoring threat but not this time. So the team will now have to play in the lower part of Pool B. Without some dual national players being added to the squad I think we may continue at that level for some time.

So that's it – 19 world championships (including play-offs), I have enjoyed being at all of them. I have made many friends, watched some excellent ice hockey and visited places I would never have considered. Hopefully there will be more opportunities in the future.

Just to add the IIHF have reported record attendances for the Pool A World Championships recently held in Prague (2015). This, of course, means my views on ticket prices do not hold water with the increased fan level.

CHAPTER 7

DEUTSCHLAND EISHOCKEY LIGA (DEL)

Having visited all the NHL arenas and completed all venues in the British Elite League, I decided to make the effort to do likewise in Germany and cover their top league, the DEL. I have again been thwarted at times with teams going bust following my visit and then playing in lower leagues i.e. Frankfurt Lions, Kassel Huskies, Essen Mosquitoes and Hannover Scorpions. In addition others have moved to new locations like Berlin, Nuremberg and Dusseldorf.

I think it is a real shame regarding the teams with financial issues. It's not just the smaller clubs either, look at the Frankfurt Lions, I remember skating at their arena before a game. They have great fans too. Surely they will return.

The standard of the DEL is excellent; speed, stick handling and a real emphasis on individual skill are all part of the teams make up. It is physical but they very rarely fight, although I have seen a few.

179

The best way to see the games is to purchase a rail pass as it really represents good value. Munich is a good place to start. I saw the Barons play some years ago in their small arena situated in the Olympic Park. With standing at both ends the atmosphere is terrific. To be honest with the standing areas it's the same throughout the league. Fan participation is just as important as the game. The Barons lost their place in the DEL a while back as the franchise was moved north to Hamburg. The Barons did continue although it was in the second league and were then promoted back to the DEL. How strange! Today they are known as the Munich Red Bulls and I have returned on several occasions to see them.

Within a 90-minute train ride from Munich there are three other DEL clubs. In Lower Bavaria is Straubing. It's a charming little town. I have been twice to watch games in their quite old arena. Boy, is it loud in there; actually the Straubing Tigers do well for a small club.

One hour in a different direction from Munich will put you in Ingolstadt. A 20-minute walk from the station brings you to the centre of town where you will find another old arena with very few seats. The Ingolstadt Panthers are another small club. I am not sure of the capacity of their rink but at the game I attended they just crammed everyone in. It was not the best viewing area.

Still in Bavaria is Augsburg, home of the Panthers (this Panthers name is quite popular). Part of the rink there is outdoors. You definitely need a few layers on; to be honest it's one of those arenas that you just feel should be hosting football. It's a few years since I was there but

I do recall seeing P.C. Drouin ice for them. I quite like the town and they have a vibrant Irish pub which I had to visit of course. My hotel seemed a little strange as it felt like a former monastery or something like that. Good to stay there though.

Moving a little further north in Bavaria will put you in Nuremberg, the home of the Ice Tigers. I have seen them play in three different arenas. The first venue was also partly outdoors and they moved to a new facility (capacity over 8,000) in 2001 which had also been built to host the World Championships. The design of this building left a lot to be desired and clearly ice hockey was not top of the agenda. On the second level it is a poor viewing area on the sides as you cannot see the whole ice pad.

On 5th January 2013 we attended the DEL Winter Classic game in Nuremberg, Ice Tigers v Eisbaren Berlin. It was played at FC Nuremberg with around 50,000 in attendance. The event was well staged but like all these games you can see very little because quite simply you are just too far away. I did enjoy the occasion though and Nuremberg is worth a visit (especially to see the Christmas Market).

Adler Mannheim (Eagles) are one of the more successful German clubs. In the southwest part of the country the town is not one of my favourites but the arena is fairly new with good viewing areas. Crowds of 8,000–10,000 are common. A tram from the centre drops you right outside the building. I have seen the Eagles play there and also a World Championship game between the Czech Republic and Canada.

Cologne Sharks (Kolner Haie) are a big city club. I mentioned the arena in the World Championship section. Along with Berlin they attract the biggest crowds in the league. From the centre of Cologne you can walk to the arena by crossing the Hohenzollern Bridge over the Rhine. On top of the bridge there are hundreds of small padlocks attached to part of the railings. These are known as lovelocks. Couples fix the padlocks then throw the key into the Rhine. This, apparently, will ensure everlasting love. I have to say this is not normally seen en route to an ice hockey game. However, If you like complete mayhem then I recommend a visit to the carnival held in Cologne in February. The fancy dress and official costumes have to be seen to be believed, drinking to excess is a must and be prepared to drink from small bottles then smash them where you stand. This is serious stuff and if there is a game later, well, that just adds to the event.

Cologne's arch rivals are Dusseldorf DEG. Its less than one hour by train. Now I can honestly say that attending a game in their old arena was the coldest I have ever been watching ice hockey. It was outside and freezing, and again it resembled a football stadium. The Metro Stars now play at a new facility. I have yet to visit but I hear the fans do not like it. The old arena may well have been freezing at times but that did not stop the terrific atmosphere they had there.

A 90-minute train ride from Cologne is Iserlohn, home of the Iserlohn Roosters, a small town club with great fans. I travelled five hours north from Straubing by train to get there one Saturday. It was actually to complete my tour of Germany. I watched a regular season game against Wolfsburg. It was just about the oldest arena I had ever been in, proper hockey, proper fans, designated drummers, what a racket they made, the NIC staff would have had kittens! I hope to visit there again.

Still within easy reach of Cologne is Krefeld. The arena is a bus ride from the station. It's actually one of the larger arenas (9,000 capacity) but it is quite unique in their catering operation.

On entry you are able to purchase a card for 10e, 15e or 20e – it's up to you. During the evening you can then just scan your card to buy food, drinks or merchandise. You may cash your card in at the end of the game or use it at the next game. This method of payment means fewer queues and quicker service. It seems to work well. Behind one of the goals at Krefeld it resembles a football style 'Kop'. The fans use it to the team's advantage by creating noise and a real partisan crowd effect. I enjoyed my evening there especially with 11 goals to watch, the Frankfurt Lions were the visitors who skated to a 7-4 win.

Travelling northeast will take you to the final three clubs in the DEL. Hamburg Freezers was my destination for a play-off game. It was actually sold out but a phone call to the club and I was assured a ticket would be reserved for me. They provided great service with a top seat in a lovely arena. The fans there love to mix with all fans and I felt very welcome. The stadium is next to the football club; from the main station it is a short train ride followed by a shuttle bus to the arena.

A Friday night in Wolfsburg was a treat, home of the gigantic VW plant, the team has an amazing name: 'Grizzly Adams Wolfsburg'. It's a small arena but it appeared bright and smart. We could not get a seat on our visit. Actually we had to follow other fans to even find it. Again, it is close to the football arena and right next to another facility which hosts handball.

We watched a play-off game against the Scorpions. It was a pulsating affair, one of a best of seven games, so we went to the next game in Hannover. After the game in Wolfsburg we ventured into the centre of town, unfortunately Wolfsburg on a Friday seemed like Nottingham on a Monday.

The final DEL team is in Berlin. There used to be two top teams there, the Capitols (West) and Eisbaren (East). I originally went to the Polar Bears old arena in the East. It held around 4,500. I recall a game there against Cologne. It was rocking with 'You'll never walk alone' and 'Ost Berlin' being belted out. A large flag (which included a small Union Jack) was passed around. There was always an edge to these fans; some of the other DEL fans dislike them. I really like going there.

Nowadays it's the O2 arena with attendances of 14,000, they provide the team with massive vocal support, and success has followed in recent years. I remember one of their players, Sven Felski, who was the ultimate in loyalty playing for one club, Berlin, for 20 years. Surely he has no equal in this and only his appearances for the German national team would see him in a different shirt. I tip my hat to him. A great sportsman!

The DEL is complete for me but wait... just like the Islanders move to Brooklyn, yet another one for me to go to. Schwenninger Wild Wings have rejoined the DEL so I need to plan a visit.

To conclude my German ice hockey tour, I need to mention the Hannover Indians who now play in the third tier of German ice hockey. It's an education to visit their arena known as the horse tower.

Firstly, drinking in the 'Jack the Ripper' bar in the city is mandatory, consuming a puck burger at the rink is a challenge, holding sparklers as the team enters the ice, well, I recall sparks falling below on a fan's head. He left only to return with a beanie hat (Indians of course) – I think health and safety left Hannover some time back. The rink is outside and it's freezing at best. Actually I have some recollection of four Indian fans visiting the NIC. It was a double header against Belfast and after each game they would go to the Castle pub. "Did you have a few beers?" I asked, of course they replied, but the first thing they ordered was four 'sticky toffee puddings'. Strange people. I have been in the company of ice hockey fans all over the world and none compare with fans of the Hannover Indians.

CHAPTER 8

CHAMPIONS HOCKEY LEAGUE (CHL)

In 2014 the IIHF launched the new Champions Ice Hockey League (CHL). It would consist of 44 teams. These clubs would come from the top leagues in Europe (the KHL was not included). The Nottingham Panthers was chosen to represent the Elite League. It would be extremely tough to say the least. They were placed in Group K along with Lukko Rauma, (Finland), Lulea Hockey (Sweden) and Hamburg Freezers (Germany).

Panthers started at home against Lukko and put up a terrific fight holding their Finnish opponents 2-2 at the end of the second period. Steve Lee scored both goals. However, two goals in the final period would see the Finns win 4-2. Craig Kowalski was in fine form. He faced 44 shots.

During this game it was plain to see just why these teams are amongst the best in Europe. Individual skill, puck retention, speed and fitness were evident. I thought the Panthers competed really well especially when you consider injuries would hit the side even that early in the season. I do not think Mark Lee ever played a shift in a Panther's shirt.

Less than 48 hours later Lulea were in town. The first period was very tight. The Swedes led 2-1 with Benedict scoring the Panthers' goal. After that, well, add clinical to what I've already said and the last two periods tell the story – a 10-1 defeat on home ice as the Swedes exploited the Panthers' weakness defensively and overall tiredness.

In the reverse fixtures a few weeks later the game followed a similar pattern. I was unable to travel although I did put together an itinerary; only personal issues prevented me attending. I watched the games via Premier Sports and Aaron Murphy. His rather quirky style has grown on me. I also like the fact he takes every opportunity to promote the British game. Relentless pressure in both games would see the Panthers lose (2-6) in Lukko and (1-9) in Lulea. The side was still missing players – Lee, Higgins and Clarke were all out which did not help.

There was a short break before the next games as the regular season started. Hamburg were the next visitors. This time the Panthers had one of those nights to remember. They stayed with their German opponents and even took the lead 2-1 in the second period through Nathan Robinson. The crowd were on their feet in the third period when K-Wall made a string of top saves, then Robert Lachowicz made it 3-1 and sealed the game when he spun around to take a pass from behind him before beating the Freezers' keeper. This goal was up there with the best I have seen – quite superb. Both sets of fans on the night were excellent.

The final CHL game would be in October in

Hamburg. I was fortunate enough to travel to Germany with some great friends and top people. It was an opportunity to celebrate my 60th birthday a little early.

We travelled the day before to allow us to see a little of the city and have a night out experiencing German food and drink. After visiting a bierkeller style bar for dinner we then ended up in rather a strange place, a water tower or something like that. It was like a round house. After walking around and around and up the tower we finally reached a really decent bar. You would never have known it was there – strange where you end up at times.

Hamburg Freezers play at the 02 arena which I had been to before; it is a train/bus ride from the centre. About 300 Panthers fans made the trip and helped to create a good atmosphere, some even joined the Freezers on the 'Kop' end and everyone was welcome. I have found this is always the way with German ice hockey fans. On the ice though Panthers were missing even more players. Clarke returned but now Benedict and Farmer were injured and Mosey was limited. Panthers went behind to a penalty shot in the first period but it was in the middle period when the Freezers went to town scoring five unanswered goals. Panthers did create some chances but fell to a 6-0 defeat and Jacina finding himself thrown out for fighting completed a poor night.

Overall, I think the club should be proud of their efforts in the CHL.

The Elite League will now have two representatives in the CHL in the 2015/16 season, Braehead and Sheffield. We wish them well and any future sides who may have the opportunity to play at this level. I will follow this competition with interest. The first winners were Lulea and in a nice touch even their fans came on to the ice to celebrate. After all, it's the fans who are always the most important in ice hockey.

190

CHAPTER 9

THE NEXT CHAPTER

The late Alan Whicker once commented that he was running out of places to visit in the world. Well in the world of ice hockey I doubt that would ever happen. Personally though I feel I do need to tick off a few more on the old bucket list. I have managed a Continental Cup final and semi-finals in the Winter Olympics and World Championships. However, the finals of the Stanley Cup beckon. Perhaps other domestic leagues in Sweden and Switzerland would be on my completion list and a visit to the KHL would present another opportunity. In addition I would very much like to attend the Spengler Cup which is held annually in Davos between Christmas and New Year.

I have always thought it would be a real challenge to visit all the AHL and ECHL clubs in North America. These are often found in backwater parts of the country. It presents a different kind of challenge. I look forward to it.

Most of all I realise how very fortunate I have been to have visited and watched so many games in different parts of the globe.

I have also made so many friends and I really hope that continues. In the unlikely event that I did ever run out of places to go and watch ice hockey, well, perhaps I could try and complete the Major League Baseball arenas (MLB). I have already managed 19 to date. Guess what though? Some have now moved to new facilities or in the case of Montreal moved cities to Washington DC, so that still leaves me with 17 to go.

Thanks for all the memories!

ACKNOWLEDGEMENTS

This is my first attempt at writing a book. I have heard it can be quite a daunting task. For me, though, I have found it an enlightening experience. In all my years at work a 'Manual Handling' booklet was probably the only claim I could make to producing anything like this. Also, it will come as no surprise that people only read that because they had to. Hopefully anyone who reads this book will find some enjoyment.

I have quite a few people to thank in helping me put together this publication.

Karen Flemming – my lovely wife, who I am sure I have managed to bore silly with all my thoughts. She is, though, a first class PA; I only had to sack her once.

William and Joan Flemming – my parents, who have always provided me with excellent support

Kevin Wright – Retired-Deputy Head Teacher – thanks for educating me in proper English, also I will never forget those marking skills.

Chris Hindson – I would have struggled to enlist help from anyone else with such extreme ice hockey knowledge.

Christine Armstrong – excellent secretarial skills.

Kevin Hindson and Martin Armstrong – thanks for your contribution.

Charlotte and Lizzie Hindson – great initiative and ideas in art and design; young children with great qualities.

Finally, to **Sassy**, our wonderful flat coat retriever, who sadly passed away in 2014. She sat with me day after day at my computer, discussing my book over a biccie. We will miss her forever.